IF ONLY SO
HAD TOL

Understanding deprived and abused children

KEN REDGRAVE

Published by the Boys' and Girls' Welfare Society 1991
Schools Hill, Cheadle, Cheshire SK8 1JE.

Typeset & printed by Manchester Free Press
Paragon Mill, Jersey Street, Manchester M4 6FP. Tel. 061-236 8822.

ISBN 1 869801 09 1

Registered Charity No. 209782.

THE PUBLISHER

The Boys' and Girls' Welfare Society is an independent charitable organisation which was founded in 1870 in Manchester. Since that time it has maintained a prominent and important role in the social and educational care of children and young people. It is actively concerned with the needs of children and young people in society, the family, and the school.

The major aims of the Society are:-

To provide appropriate residential care and education for deprived, disadvantaged, handicapped or emotionally disturbed children and young people.

To provide, assist, or participate in community based care and education projects for the benefit of the deprived, disadvantaged, and/or handicapped in society.

To initiate and promote research and publication in the field of social and educational care.

To promote and participate in complementary co-operative ventures in social work and education.

To improve professional standards in those caring professions concerned with children and young people.

This book is dedicated to
JUNE OGDEN
An inspired and inspiring
child care worker

ACKNOWLEDGEMENTS

I would like to acknowledge John McG McMaster for his general guidance in this work, Pauline Bruchez and Susan Lamonby for their scrutiny and advice. Also, Sheila Redgrave for her typing of the original manuscript.

CONTENTS

PREFACE

In recent years many of us have been dismayed over the number of moves many children have experienced in the twelve, eight or even only five years of their lives. These moves or 'placements' as the jargon has it, are not simply the geographical household moves of the family so common these days in our Western society, due to parents 'moving house' on account of job changes and, often, promotion.

No — the moves I am talking of here are the **transfers** from one family, or children's centre, to another family or some other 'placement'. In these moves, the child may lose not only friends and the school she has become used to, but the parents or people who are acting as parents. Worse still, she may gradually lose self-esteem, trust in others, and even the desire to relate closely to anyone at all in a special child-parent way. So I am talking, here, about the damaging and negative effects these many moves may have on the development of the personality.

It is the **number** of moves a child may have whilst 'in care' that is so distressing. Clearly, if we can help a child by removing him to a caring environment, where the previous environment has failed that child, and where the chances of rehabilitation (in the widest sense) are poor, so much to the good. But where I find a child of say ten years, who has had seventeen, twenty, or as with one child I met, twenty-seven placements (parents, relatives, foster homes, children's homes, etc. etc.) then it seems to me that the care agencies have lost their way and the child has become a parcel and is heading for mental health disaster.

Yet I cannot usually find that individuals have been blame-worthy on account of negative attitudes. The histories of these children are strewn with good intentions. Often the people who wish to help older children, by which I mean children over about five years of age, do not appreciate either the extent of the damage previous placements have caused, or the psychological harm of the **poor** early-infancy nurture they have received. Nor do they expect the problems they eventually encounter.

The main title of this book 'If Only Someone Had Told Me' reflects the anguish and feelings of failure so often expressed after a fostering or adoption placement has broken down ('disrupted') and in the three chapters of the book I try in the first place to describe in everyday language the sort of children and teenagers needing help. This is done in Chapter One by simply using a set of portraits or pen-picture descriptions of eleven young people.

Then, in the following two chapters I have briefly outlined some causes of behaviour and personality factors. Caregivers (foster parents, adopters, residential and day-care workers) are likely to experience such behaviour and personality traits in the children. So Chapter Two looks at what has been **missing** from their lives, whilst Chapter Three looks at what deleterious experiences were **included.**

What this particular work does not attempt is to outline care or therapeutic treatment programmes, but perhaps on the foundation of the present volume, such an outline may emerge in the form of a subsequent work. However, it is to be hoped that there will be found clear indicators in the body of the present text concerning care and placement policies for such children as I have described.

Throughout the book I have used both masculine and feminine personal pronouns, sometimes referring to she/her and at other times to he/him. To me this seems more natural than sticking all the way through, to one or the other.

Apart from the quotations from biographical books in which the author has described him or herself or has named and described real people, the descriptions of children and adults in this book, notably in Chapter One, do not describe actual individuals, child or adult. I have drawn upon oft repeated situations and circumstances so that, although none of the descriptions represents a real person, they all strongly reflect **typical** children and circumstances.

I hope that, as well as foster and adoptive parents (actual and prospective) this book will help many students of child care, social workers, teachers, doctors, policy-makers, and **children** in care.

CHAPTER ONE

All Shapes and Sizes

Stephen

He likes to be called Stevey. He is now in another Children's Home. I say **another** home because this is his third experience of residential care, but he also has had six, yes **six,** foster family placements. As a matter of fact, the professionals don't call this place, **Barclay House,** a Children's Home. They hardly use that term at all now; they call it a **Family Centre.** But I use the term Children's home because that's what Stevey calls it.

Stevey is hanging about in the centre just now because he has been 'suspended' from school. You probably wouldn't think of Stevey as likely to be suspended — 'expelled' he said. You would think it even less likely that the reason for this punishment was his 'attack' on a female teacher.

Stevey is an attractive twelve-year old who may, and usually does, greet people with a lovely smile and will immediately pay attention to their needs, asking 'who do you want to see?' Would they like a chair? Would they like a cup of tea while they wait? If the facilities were to hand Stevey would make the pot of tea or coffee and bring it along on a tray, and pour out the brew for our guest — very impressive and endearing. Fancy suspending him from school!

Tears come easily to Stevey. He has been recently involved in some special **preparation work,** that is to say a counselling situation in which a professional worker aims to help him overcome some of his **hang-ups.** This work involves helping the child to sort out his own history and feelings. Many children remain dry-eyed even though they are sometimes in a heightened emotional state during the sessions, but not Stevey. Stevey has a silent weep. He might be engaged in drawing a memory picture of some place or incident, and the worker suddenly notices that the paper is getting wet from Stevey's silent tears. Some people say he 'turns them on'.

How do you feel when your own mother says to you that she hates you? Maybe that happens a lot when people are grown up, but it could feel different coming from Mum when you are only five or six years old. How does it feel when your mother makes you walk two or three yards behind her when out shopping and you are six years old? That is what happened to Stevey. His mother told him that she did not want people to know that he was hers when she walked out with him!

You could say that all Stevey's early childhood training was training (or brainwashing) to implant the idea, and the feelings associated with the idea, that he was totally useless — **rubbish!**

Every time Stevey moved, either into a new foster family or a residential 'establishment' he felt he wanted it 'to work', but he always took with him the feelings and the ideas that his parents had implanted in him about his being rubbish. His father, incidentally, also refused to own him saying that he couldn't be **his son** because he was not 'macho' enough, he was 'Cissy'.

Nearly always there was some other kid around, in whichever family he joined, who would somehow remind Stevey that what his parents had said must be true. These children were always felt as a terrible threat. Stevey did not say they were a menace, even when talking silently to himself. He wanted to own this family, not get 'kicked out'. But the closer he tried to get to the adults, or to one of them, the stronger this feeling became. It was a feeling which seemed to talk to him and to say 'This other kid is having more than me' or 'I'm not sure, but I think he's having more love than I am'. And Stevey would find himself doing something to make the other child feel like **he** felt when his parents rejected him. Then the other kid, as like as not, would start hating him. Sometimes Stevey would have to do something just to see if that would happen. Sometimes he found a way of keeping one of the foster parents to himself, perhaps by being nasty to the other one. But gradually they all seemed to get the same idea as his parents, and as other foster parents and teachers had got — the idea that Stevey was **rubbish.** Then he would have to go. And when he moved on he felt even more like **rubbish** than when he first went there.

Some people described all this as 'manipulative'. They said to each other and in their reports 'This child is manipulative'. Of course it is easy to say all this and to make the foster parents or the staff of the centre seem like insensitive and hopeless people who should not be caring for disturbed kids, but it is not as simple as that. The other side of the coin is that Stevey **does** cause other children to become unhappy. He **does** say nasty things about them or their parents in order to get them worked up. The whole chemistry, so to speak, of families, gets churned up. Even in the Children's Home the staff find him very difficult, and so very demanding of attention. How can you give the likes of Stevey the attention he requires when you have twelve other children to cope with and fights are breaking out!

The staff know that many of Stevey's 'tantrums' are due to his feelings of jealousy of other children, especially when he sees them moving out into foster and adoptive families or returning to their own parents. Sometimes these feelings get mixed up with the 'I'm rubbish' feelings.

When Stevey is stopped from doing something, or when told that he cannot have whatever he is asking for he is likely to feel that this is **because** of him being himself — anyone else would have got 'yes' for an answer. Then he is likely to 'pull silly faces' as someone put it. School situations are dangerous because then there may be thirty other kids watching and Stevey boils up inside himself if he is 'shown up'. That is why he pushed past the teacher. That is why he clumsily bumped against a projector screen and sent it crashing on to her head and, when she got very cross and grabbed him by the collar, that is why he kicked her and slapped her across the face — that is why he finished up 'suspended' from school.

Stevey is quite musical. Recently he has begun to feel a bit better about himself, at least in one small area of his life. Never before was anyone prepared to spend time training him to play an instrument or to encourage him. He has recently started learning on a keyboard instrument. It has been a discovery. He is really quite artistic and sensitive.

Also he knows now that it is O.K. for him to have a hug or a cuddle, even at twelve years of age. Stevey is beginning, just beginning, to lose a tiny bit of the **rubbish** feeling.

* * * * *

I would like to introduce you to eleven children — perhaps I should say children and young adults, since there are fifteen-and sixteen-year olds amongst them. Steven is one of these children.

I could have introduced you to dozens of children, but I felt twelve would be enough to be going on with. When you have been introduced to these children, and it is only an introduction, I would like to share with you some thoughts about how they, and many other children, have turned out to be so 'difficult to cope with' and so demanding.

We shall have to take a look at the way children develop, and the things which are important in their development.

These pen-pictures of children, and the discussions in the following chapters, may go some way in making up for the small amount of information **child caregivers** have had in the past. By the expression child caregivers I mean foster parents, adoptive parents, natural parents and anyone in fact who is bringing up or teaching, or helping a child who may have experienced a disturbing and disruptive past. I hope also that people who are considering caring for such a child will benefit from meeting the rest of the children to be introduced in a moment. Perhaps then we shall not have distressed caregivers saying, when things have gone 'hopelessly' wrong; 'If only someone had told me!'

Sally

There are some dogs that go mad crazy whenever you call on their owners. Maybe they are not very well trained, maybe they are untrainable, but the result is that almost before you have got through the door they are at you. You are slapped about by their tongues, slobbered over by their 'kisses', crushed by their paws (they are usually huge hounds with prodigious strength) bowled over by their hind quarters, and lashed with their tails. It is as if they are starved of all affection and must 'devour' you. Having at last been threatened with extinction unless they desist, and are settled uneasily on the rug, one misplaced glance in their direction, and the whole crazy love scene starts all over again.

This is the impression I sometimes get of Sally. Sally seems never to be able to obtain enough overt affection to satisfy her needs. It is the same when she's at home or at school, or if she visits your home or attends a party. There is a sort of hunger all the time for demonstrative affection.

There's another characteristic about this eight year old child. She always wants to be 'babied'. At school she still wants to be the 'baby' and play in the Wendy House. The other kids can be the

'Mums and Dads' and so forth, but she wants to be the baby.

She knows some real babies and often wants to play a game where she is a particular baby. 'I'm baby Joe' or 'baby Caroline' she says. 'You put me in the bed and sing me to sleep ------------ call me Caroline'.

Sally is an intellectually (or cognitively) 'normal' child, she is not educationally retarded in a way which would categorise her for any special schooling or streaming although she is right at the bottom of her class at school. She is fairly active. She's a chatterbox and likes to sing and dance, but is always hungry for the attention of adults, men and women. Some people say she's 'all out for Number One', and indeed she watches any share-out of sweets like a hawk watching its prey — **and** she pounces if she thinks anyone's come off better than she has.

Strangely enough, despite the dog-like readiness to swamp adults with affection, in return for affection, and the 'baby' behaviour, Sally also becomes a nuisance on account of a bossy streak she has where other children are concerned. 'She **will** take over ...... **and** she's got quite a mind of her own and can be quite defiant' people say. Naturally, she loses her 'friends'. Kids don't want to come and play when all they get are orders to 'Be the nurse and wash me ------ or some such instruction. Everything Sally does **looks** very deliberate. I don't say it is deliberate, I only say it looks like it. So you get people saying that she **deliberately** wets her pants. She goes on and on playing, when she could quite easily go to the lavatory, then **swish** 'she just stands there and does it!'

An alternative to bossing is Sally's withdrawal or isolate behaviour. This may happen when any of her friends have been invited round to play with her. She will completely ignore them and maybe go and play with her computer in her room.

I suppose Sally is an example of what some people like to describe as 'a survivor'. A number of other interesting descriptions seem to have accompanied her through life so far. One which appears quite early in her medical records and in the Social Services Department file is 'non-organic failure to thrive', NOFT for short. Quite a lot of children who are referred to hospital on account of failure to grow, turn out to have no illness (as yet) causing the lack of growth, but to have related social and psychological impediments. Sally was in and out of hospital during her first two years of life for various actual ailments, such as pneumonia, and jaundice, but then she still failed for some time to grow (or to **thrive**) even after overcoming illnesses.

At about four years of age she finished up in a Children's Home run by a voluntary society. At around six years old she was placed with her present foster parents.

There is a deep sense of being unfulfilled which permeates Sally's life. It is not that, at this moment, she lacks amenities in her life style. Compared with many children in the third world she must be well off, rolling in riches and comfort. The actual house she lives in is clean and bright, surrounded by gardens. She has plenty of toys and much of the more sophisticated paraphernalia associated with childhood today, including a computer with computerized games in her 'software' department. She goes to Brownies, and sometimes to the roller-rink and has birthday parties and family holidays.

None of this provides whatever it is that will take away that feeling of emptiness and give her that filled-up feeling she gets when she plays at 'babies' or when occasionally, an adult holds her on her (or his) lap and reads a story to her.

But when this does happen Sally is made to feel she's doing something odd. Something a 'big girl' like her should not need to do. For some reason her foster mother has never felt able to hold or nurse Sally. In fact she hardly likes to touch her. 'Big girls don't sit on laps and suck thumbs'. But the feeling inside Sally says 'forget you're a big girl — push in and get a kiss from that lady--------- see if Uncle Richard will pick you up--- ------- Oh no, it's not fair, why does Samantha get loved all the time and I don't?'

All the restricting and trying to hold her back seems to have little effect. And she always bobs up again almost immediately after a telling off. As a matter of fact **telling-offs** do not seem to have much effect, 'Like water on a duck's back---------- goes in one ear and out of the other! ---------- Now look what you've done to that dress! ---------- Right, go upstairs and get ready for bed'.

Robert

'He's buggered off again, the bastard, and I'm not keeping this one ------'

'You can't leave 'im 'ere ------- what'll yer dad say?' 'I couldn't care less what 'e bloody well says ------ I've been up all night with this one, crying and banging 'is 'ead on the cot side ----- I can't cope.'

Debbie Calvert, mother of Robert aged eighteen months and now carrying her second, was all for planting Robert for the third time with her own mother. Her second cohabittee, not the father of

Robert, had, in her words, 'buggered off again'. Debbie was just eighteen and a half years old.

'Take 'im up the Welfare', said her Mum, 'I'm not 'aving 'im left on my 'ands again while you drink yourself into 'ospital ------ you've only just been dried out'.

'I'll leave 'im 'ere while I go up the Welfare then ------ shut up yer little bugger ------stop crying and I'll bring yer some sweeties ------ God my mouth's like a sewer'.

That all happened a long time ago in Robert's life. It is different now. He is in care and in a foster home. This is his fourth foster home and tenth placement. The other times he was in Children's Homes. Some people are embarrassed by him. Some are irritated. The kids at school first made fun of him and then, as he slapped them down with his tongue and bossed them about, and boasted of his general superiority of knowledge and experience they turned against him.

Robert is now a gangling thirteen-year old. He is a nice enough looking lad and he has an above average vocabulary for his age. This made the kids at school call him a 'snob'. Now we all know something about mentally handicapped children, and these days people appreciate their developmental problems and are not surprised about them playing 'baby games' ------ even other kids 'understand them'. But Robert is not 'handicapped', nor is he classified as requiring special educational help. He presents as a normal thirteen year old who has been brought up in a 'nice' family. He can hold an intelligent conversation. Perhaps this is why, when he wants to play with little toys typical of those favoured by six-year-olds, or even four year olds, some adults tend to become irritated or embarrassed. They get especially embarrassed when Robert suddenly experiences something as exciting or pleasing, perhaps on an outing, and, as a result of some sort of reflex action, jumps up and down, whoops loudly, claps his hands, or laughs in an exaggerated and 'silly' fashion. Not only does Robert like playing with 'little kiddy' toys such as motor cars, tiny dolls, and plastic soldier boys, but he only really enjoys playing with children much younger than his own peer group. He gravitates, to use a word often used by adults in his life, towards children of eight or nine years old.

He is not a happy child, this thirteen-year old. He comes across, as they say, when you first meet him, as unnaturally domesticated and oozing courtesy and the 'polite' mannerisms of the middle class. But it's all part of the facade — the act! It hides a smouldering anger, a bitterness about life.

Some people experience a different Robert. The one behind the facade. School teachers and other children in his class are liable to meet with a vicious round of verbal abuse and with accusations of favouritism; 'You always take **their** side ---- I hate you' or with a suggestion that everyone is plotting against him; 'They always leave me all the old broken tools to use ------ --'

School reports often caricature Robert: 'Attention span very short if left unattended ------ demands attention from the teacher ------ has done some good work on occasions but spoils himself by silly, noisy behaviour in class ------ disrupts other children ------ has no friends'.

'I wish I could find out what is going on in his mind' said his foster mother.

We tend to think about behaviour that way. There is something going on in that kid's mind, and whatever it is, whatever ideas or thoughts he has — are making him act out in some way. That's probably true to a great extent.

But behind Robert's thoughts are **feelings.** Feelings he can never express in words, not because he hasn't a big enough vocabulary but because the feelings are so very private or because they cause so much pain, or because he tries to hide them from himself. Even if he wanted to say how he felt he wouldn't be able to get it out. Instead, what comes out is something do with other feelings. Instead of the crying, sad feelings, out comes something to do with the angry 'get lost' feeling.

'Fancy a great big lad like that clinging on to his father' said an onlooker watching Robert with his foster father at a party --- --- 'he's all of five foot ten'. That's another thing, Robert stands out like a skyscraper from the rest of the kids in his age group so he looks like a fifteen year old, an oddly behaving fifteen year old!

If you were to ask Robert why he 'clings', which would be a pain-causing thing to do, he would say 'I don't know'. If kids ask him to play with them he may say; 'I'm not interested in joining in your game of cricket or football, I just want to sit here' (next to mum or dad!) or some such statement.

Robert experiences many feelings which make him 'cling' as people put it. Some of these feelings are so basic that they've been there all the time, as far back as he can remember. They have got something to do with the way little twelve-month or eighteen-month old toddlers feel and behave in the presence of strangers or some vaguely threatening situation. The toddler heads for Mum or Dad and holds on. It's as though Robert got 'stuck' somehow at that age as far as that bit of **feeling** goes, while all sorts of other bits of him 'grew up'.

Sometimes people say he's 'clinging' but the truth is that he is avoiding some painful situation or experience which nobody but himself seems to know is painful or dangerous. You see he is terribly scared of so many things which other kids are not scared of, and the rules about being a boy, and being 'a man' don't allow you to be scared of such tings. He has got one terrible secret, he is dead scared of matches, and he is dead clumsy so that when he **has** actually tried to light a match he has burnt his fingers and become even more scared. Cricket balls are deadly things to Robert, dangerous beyond imagination. 'Get out of our game Robert', you're no flipping good — you're rubbish!'

At school Robert cannot of course go and sit next to mum and dad. He tried sitting next to a teacher and starting a conversation about something he knows all about — motor cars — but it didn't work. For various reasons, including these scarey feelings, and boasting, cover-up feelings resulting in 'You all hate me' and 'I'll smash your face in' feelings, he is either excluded from the games of other kids or feels too uncomfortable to join in - he **'Hates'** physical education. So Robert sits inside, alone, during playtime. He withdraws. And his school report says; 'Robert is a loner'.

Michelle

Michelle keeps changing her personality! Not in the normal way people do as they grow older, but in a disconcerting way. In fact, in a worrying way. One time she will be a chatty, bright eyed little girl ready to play. Six months later people are saying that she only uses two or three words, and is cowed and retiring. One time she will be a child who sleeps peacefully at night times, and three months later she's a little girl who not only cannot sleep at nights but who screams and bangs her head against the hardest object she can find, including the wall if it is reachable. She deliberately hurts herself in other ways, sometimes pulling her own hair or slapping her own face. She is nearly three years old.

Michelle has experienced long periods when life has had a totally different feeling about it from other periods of her life experience. These different **feeling** periods are long to her, but in fact they vary from two months to six months and have been going on ever since she can remember, and in reality ever since she was born. If any child has been tossed on the ocean waves of life,

Michelle is such a child. In her short period of life she has been constantly in and out of care, and in and out of hospital.

There are people, grown ups, who come and go and seem to her to coincide with these chunks of different feelings. When the people come and go there are different things and different places that come and go with them. Michelle feels frightened and happy, anxious and secure, and troubled and peaceful all at the same time, though sometimes the frightened feeling is big and the secure feeling is little, whilst at other times the happy feeling is big and the troubled feeling is -----? still there, but a long way away. Then it begins to creep nearer, and suddenly it pounces.

When Michelle has these different feelings in these different places with these different people she does different things, or the same things in a different way. Sometimes some of the grown- ups, usually the same ones, shout at her because she's done the thing in the 'wrong' way --- in the way she is supposed to do it in the other place with the other people. Life for Michelle is very dangerous and very distracting — you can easily, in her life, do the thing 'wrong' simply because you do the 'right' thing in the wrong place — with the wrong people!

Michelle has devised ways of keeping the troubled feeling from creeping up too quickly, or for beating off this frightened feeling and hanging on to the secure feeling, but none of her tricks are very successful, and there is always the possibility of the dangerous feelings pouncing quite suddenly accompanied by dangerous people who have tremendous power over her.

Let me give you a pen-picture of Michelle when she first went to a 'short-term' foster family, the Ruddocks. She was almost two years of age then. She made no attempt to relate to anyone in the Ruddock family, nor to anyone else. She showed no ability to play in any way either with toys, children, or grown-ups. She would crawl aimlessly about the floor, even if toys were present. Like so many children who have been shuttled from one belongingness to another, or to and from belongingness mingled with rejection, she at first did not seem to react to pain and discomfort as we expect children to. To the onlooker it was as if she didn't feel pain and discomfort to the usual degree. If an older child pedalled over her hand on his tricycle, or wolloped her on the face with his fist she would not flinch. If she was wet, and she often was because she was still in nappies, she would ignore it. Even when she appeared to have a nappy rash she would not protest.

Sometimes though, Michelle's body seemed to protest all on its own. It was as if it had decided to go on strike and not grow any more. This happened when she was only eighteen months old, and then again when she was about two and a half years old. Both times she went to hospital and the doctors and nurses gave her special foods and drinks which should have made her grow taller and put on weight, but she didn't. Everything stood still. Being there, having special food and being loved by the nurses felt good and bad at the same time to her. No-one could quite say why her body was behaving in this way. Nobody could find an illness. The doctors said it was 'Non-Organic Failure to Thrive'. Which is simply a special way of saying that her body had gone on strike.

So far as Michelle was concerned, she knew nothing about failure to thrive but she did know about frightened feelings and the **being lost** or **gone away** feelings. Sometime she felt she was lost even when she was in hospital. She also felt she had lost people who had been caring for her. There was something bad about people who were there at one time, being warm and cuddling you, or even shouting at you, but still being there, and then **not** being there. There was something frightening about these people because they had something to do with this 'don't want you any more' feeling. They had something to do with this thing inside her which made her feel angry at the same time as she wanted to be loved.

Although Michelle had no words to describe her mixture of feelings she was really experiencing the world as a place that could not be trusted. Although she could not explain any of this, she knew that if she did certain things to her body she could make strong physical feelings come, feelings which were so strong they could cut out the thinking feelings and leave her only with her body feelings. This was one reason for her head-banging and pulling her own hair. This was why she did not react to pain in the way we expect children to react. But there were other feelings she could make. She could make a special feeling come down low where her legs met. This was why she openly masturbated.

Now at the time of writing, Michelle has changed again. In fact I am now seeing two Michelles because she is going to and from her foster home and to and from the home of her parents and siblings (who are also bouncing in and out of care). At home Michelle is head-banging and unable to sleep at nights. She is refusing to eat any food. She has started to soil again and needs to be in nappies, and she has stopped talking except to use a very basic set of words. Michelle in fact regresses at home, yet she will often cling to her mother and even become 'poorly' with a temperature and flushed face. After a few days at home, she develops dark shadows under her eyes.

Then, when she has been in her 'short-term' foster home for two or three weeks, I meet the other Michelle who recently, whilst in the foster home, has been able to play and to talk. She's still, even in the foster home, a very insecure little girl who will behave in all sorts of unusual and occasionally alarming ways with people. She will sometimes rip her clothes up. She cannot stand being teased and will exhibit violent behaviour if pushed very far. Instead of refusing food she is a compulsive eater who will go on and on stuffing it down, if its there in front of her, until she vomits. Strangest of all, if her foster parents are occupied and she's left to 'play' on her own, she will gradually become still and listless and probably lie on the floor, gradually losing all movement. Even her breathing reduces to almost nil — Michelle has turned on a strong cataleptic condition, and may have to be rocked back to 'life'.

John

I met John first in a police cell. He was on remand and awaiting a court hearing. He should have been sent to some other place 'more suitable' for holding sixteen year olds, but it was said that there were no vacancies, so John sat in a cell. It looked to me as though years of 'punishment' stretched ahead. After all, he had already spent a year in a secure unit, and before that he had been in special units, and schools for maladjusted children.

'What these lads need is a good thrashing' said an acquaintance of mine on reading the local newspaper account of 'YOUTH ACCUSED OF BURGLARY AND MALE PROSTITUTION'. She did not know it was John, of course. 'Do them a world of good if they put them in the army - make men of them' she said.

From the very beginning of his life John had experienced punishment. Not just the odd tap on the hand but brutal punishment. Punishment for John seemed to have been a built-in characteristic of the universe. It wasn't only that physical punishment was practised upon him by sadistic people, though that was damaging enough. Circumstances, chance if you like, seemed to have ganged up against him. His mother died two months after he was born. At six months of age he went into hospital because of 'failure to thrive'. In the hospital he contracted hepatitis.

Whilst he was in hospital his father was sent to prison for 'procuring' children for prostitution, so that on leaving hospital at ten months old John went to a foster family. He really should have been protected by being made a Ward of Court or by some other statutory protective measure, but just at that time the popular press was having a campaign against social workers who took children from parents, so the Social Services Department duly recorded him as being 'At Risk' but left him available for when his father returned to normal life and freedom.

This book is not the place to recount all the punishing events in John's childhood, but they went on and on. Now he is 'awaiting a further placement'. The social worker's report, made whilst John was still in the secure unit, gives a pen-picture of this youth insofar as his behaviour is concerned although, understandably, it says nothing about his feelings.

John, the report states, cannot let people get 'close' to him, that is to say, close in terms of friendship or warmth of feeling. As a matter of fact a much earlier report about John when he was twelve years old also pointed out that he 'rejects any attempt to cuddle him or even put one's arm around his shoulder'. It goes on to say that 'this child seems to be incapable of giving expression to his feelings although his childhood is filled with situations normally giving rise to sadness, remorse and fear ------'

I know now, because messages have come to me from John in a very indirect way, that there is a great and frightening feeling which has to do with destruction and punishment, and which comes from somewhere inside people 'who get close to you'. I know also that there are times when he has got feelings of frustration and failure (he often fails at things). There are times when he feels drawn towards **punishing** someone or something. It is as if others must feel what he feels. If others are hurt like he feels hurt; if others feel pain and stop being jolly, or sympathetic, or just carrying on with their own things, then maybe John will feel - satisfied? He's not quite sure what he expects to feel. I don't think he has ever really experienced joy or even freedom from jealousy. John keeps testing, that's the word **testing.** Testing for response in people. Vaguely he feels that he ought to be able to know a different feeling; what people talk about when they 'like' someone, he will not think about that other thing, 'loving' someone. It is too dangerous — too stupid.

Things can be hurt as well as people. Sometimes you can combine hurting things with hurting people. John once helped to set fire to a school building. Fire is special. Fire has got something to do with the feelings that used to come up inside him when he had cigarette ends stubbed out on him at eight years old. It has also something to do with his present feelings. Fire consumes. Fire gets out of control easily; fire is both comforting and frightening — like his father; like his feelings.

John is gay. Lots of men have 'had' John. When he was little lots of men had him. John's father has trained him to have men. His father and he now work together in a run-down inner-city area. His father procures — he is John's pimp — and John satisfies the customers. There is only his father who, apart from 'the men', seems to see him as in any way **special.** This is a strange relationship and John has 'funny' dreams about himself and his father because there is a lot of hatred and guilt mixed up in all this, but yet John feels they **belong** together, especially now. It was different when John was little. He sometimes imagined then that he wanted a mother, but now, with all the enemies around like the police, the social workers, and the magistrates, they can share the fight together, him and his dad.

Anyway, John says he does **enjoy** what he and the men do. At one time he felt about it much in the same way as the other brutal treatment he received. But now he feels sort of 'special' to the men, or to some of them.

Only when he is alone, like now, in the cell and at night time does he have another feeling — a sad feeling. He often has the same dream then, all about a woman, a very big sort of giant woman who cries, and begins to crush him with her bosom. He has awakened to find himself crying — crying! The shame of it.

'Yes, that's what they need', said my wealthy lady acquaintance 'a damn good hiding — teach them a lesson'.

Morag

I think that in our modern industrialised 'Western' society Morag will always need to be 'protected' to some extent. This need not be protection by statutory powers or by 'the Authorities', but under the circumstances it could come to that. I have known young people who shared some of Morag's disabilities and who eventually married and found all the care and protection they needed from the marriage. To be honest, I think that only worked where the 'normal' partner, man or woman, carried a stronger **parenting** role than is carried by most married people towards their partner, but it can work out that way, and I imagine it could happen in Morag's life. She is now fifteen years old.

It is generally agreed that Morag is pretty and has a lot of charm. She has a lovely smile and very easily makes friends. At least, that is the impression she gives, and to some extent it is true, but she has many other facets to her personality, some of which I shall describe. This business of being **friendly,** for example. How does it come about that Morag may very well end up being the central hate-figure and scapegoat in a fracas involving a crowd of peer group mates, male and female, but usually female?

It is true that Morag desires to like everyone. But the other side of the coin is that she is desperate for everyone to like her, and to **show** that they like her. Not only does she want this two-way display of acceptance and overt display of 'kindness' but she really cannot stand anyone in her circle of relatives, friends or acquaintances showing any kind of disagreement within the circle. All concerned must **love** one another and be kind and generous and understanding. The inevitable tiffs between members generate enormous emotional stress in Morag who then strives, with her limited competence, to reduce the damage, patch up the quarrels, or keep both (or several) members happy by verbal balancing tricks.

I referred just now to Morag's **limited competence.** In fact competence, or ability, is spread completely unevenly throughout her personality. To be with her for any length of time is like being with half a dozen children of assorted ages, ranging from five to fifteen years old. Here is a fifteen year old girl who will harp on one subject for a whole hour, or longer, and who one moment is asking 'where was your soul before you were born - before you were a baby?' and shortly after is asking 'how big is an ant to a man?' Here is a fifteen year old who cannot grasp the meaning of honesty or understand how to use a can-opener; who cannot understand clearly what is meant by the term **marriage,** for example, but who is able to figure out the square-root of a three figure number almost as quickly as a calculator. So when I talk about her limited competence you will appreciate that I am simplifying my description somewhat.

However, in coping with people and life in general Morag finds great difficulty. In many ways she is a little child apt to get lost, literally lost, if sent on a 'message' or asked to go shopping locally. She is likely to be found crying, lost, somewhere, and to be brought back by the police. Yet she desperately wants to 'grow up' and be like other girls of her age.

So much does she want to be **normal** (my word, not hers) and to be accepted that she strives to reflect the fashions and absorb the ideas of her peer group, no matter what happens to be the moral or social tone of the group. Unfortunately her time is spent between a 'residential home with education on the premises' an adult ward of a hospital, and two 'holiday fostering placements'. She also has access at different times to both her parents, both of whom are patients in psychiatric wards.

In the Residential Home with Education Morag feels that what girls of her age should have are 'boy friends'. Other, intellectually (but not morally) more stable girls egg her on, for the fun mileage, telling her how slow she is and what she ought to be doing with boys. This leads to long discussions between Morag and her social worker on what boys want, what they should have sexually, and what they have actually obtained sexually from her, and also to the administering of 'contraceptive pills' supplied to Morag as a result of case conferences and doctor's prescriptions.

It is very easy to get poor Morag behaving in an obsessional manner. She nearly starved herself to a skeleton recently on account of a gum abscess which required dental surgery and left her in pain when eating. Once having experienced such pain, and all the hullabaloo surrounding her dental surgery, she flatly refused to eat anything for days and days. There was another time when she insisted on wearing a woollen hat all the time, indoors and out — nobody could persuade her to take it off.

At night times, in the Residential Home, she cannot sleep. This is partly on account of the cruel teasing from other girls, who tell her that there are 'bogy-men' about, and partly because she wets the bed and gets into a state.

So much does Morag want to be in the running, that she frequently comes out with lurid descriptions of things (often sexual) which have happened to her. It is extremely difficult to distinguish between those that have really happened and those that have not happened. However, in certain settings for example, in the holiday foster homes, all such talk ceases, and Morag becomes enthusiastic about the ideas that prevail there and the life styles practised.

Morag may panic, really panic. I'm not using this term in a loose way now, I am referring to the things that happen to her body when fear strikes. Of course the fears are about 'perfectly silly' things as many adults tell her, but that does not prevent the cramps grabbing her in the stomach, or her heart from beating like a pop group gone beserk, or sweat coming all over her forehead.

Sometimes Morag is misunderstood, and misunderstands at the same time. Really on these occasions the messages are just not getting across from one person to the other. Sometimes, in fact, completely false messages are received — messages which neither Morag nor the other person intended to send out. Take the one about being touched by boys. Morag wrote a sort of poem in which she was asking, desperately it seemed, for a boy to **touch** her. She put this poem up on the wall for all to see, especially for Stuart to see. It was quite understandable that the lady in charge of the group should take Morag on one side about this dangerous invitation since there had been other poems even more salacious — Morag was asking for it. But confusion followed.

Morag had once, when she was ten, been assured that **all** boys and men were out to 'get' her. She became obsessional about this. Recently she'd been 'desensitised' on this point and had learnt that dancing with a boy and therefore being 'touched' (in a proper way) was O.K. — so why couldn't she ask for a boy to 'touch' her now she'd learnt that it was O.K.? I will not labour this little episode, but believe me there was so much confusion!

Morag is many people. Morag is sweet, and gentle, and adores people. She loves everyone around to be loving and kind and happy, and full of song. Where there is such an atmosphere, or one approaching it (none can be perfect!) she remains a happy child in a charmed world. 'But sometimes I see men fighting on the T.V. and the girls are all arguing near me, and I feel I want to fight'.

Judy and Tony

This is their third foster home. Judy and Tony have been in care for about a year. The social workers are still trying to keep them together so that they will grow up as siblings usually do, experiencing the close relationship of at least one blood relative.

Whenever a sibling group come into care people think to themselves 'keep them together'. This is understandable, and laudable, but there are instances when, to keep too rigidly to that first reflexive thought will ensure a series of fostering breakdowns.

However, Judy and Tony are living together. Their first foster home was intended only as a short-term placement and was intended to be a 'holding' and preparation place whilst a long-term family, possibly 'long term with a view to eventual adoption', was found for them,

They both come into care rather suddenly and, so far as they were concerned, unexpectedly. Tony in fact was in bed when the social workers arrived. Well, he'd been naughty. As a matter of factual recording he'd been 'On my nerves all day long — and you know how noise affects me!' (his mothers words). Judy was still up even though it was nearly eleven p.m. She is eight and Tony is nine years old.

After being in care for about six months they were introduced to 'a new family', the Burrows. The placement lasted exactly five weeks. Why? Why did it break down so quickly? By the way, most of the professionals involved did not say it had 'broken down', they said it had **disrupted.** Judy and Tony had some odd feelings about **disruption,** not that they used that word of course.

Judy was so confused! She hadn't wanted to leave her parents. True, she had been most unhappy at home and had often been terrified at the rows going on downstairs between them. True her mother seemed to hate her, no matter what she did to appease and to keep the peace between her parents. But in this foster family it seemed that parents did not fight and argue. But they gave strange looks to each other at times, as much as to say 'What's she up to now'.

At home she had learnt special things to do so as to be loved by her father. He had taught her some things himself as well. She learnt some of these things when she was quite young — only about four years old. But when she'd tried the same things out with Mr. Burrows, things she thought she ought to do so as to be loved, he had got all worked up and a bit huffed and told her to get off his lap, and she'd heard them talking about it afterwards in whispers, and the social worker came. All she'd done was to work herself up and down putting one of her legs between his, like her dad had told her.

You could not blame the Burrows. This was not what they had expected when they agreed to take the children. They had three children of their own, and apart from what Judy 'got up to' they had been horrified at Tony's behaviour with their children. And his language! And the words he used! Mrs. Burrows had to use just the initial letters when she spoke to the social worker about Tony.

The whole thing made Mrs. Burrows 'ill' and Mr. Burrows distracted. The family was being destroyed. Then there were the neighbours, and the neighbours' children. There was a terrible shindy the time nice Mrs. Harper found Tony lying on top of her six-year old daughter and trying to put his 'willie' up her.

Tony was immediately labelled as a 'sex maniac', but that wasn't all. He was also very aggressive towards other children, and he had a 'streak of cruelty in him'. To get his own back, and to get the feeling of being 'big and strong and important' he had dug a deep hole in the back garden and had attempted to bury alive, Mrs. Harper's cat!

Sleep flew away from the Burrow's household. Feelings of anger, despair, guilt and incredulity took its place. And there was talk, talk, talk far into the night. Tony and Judy had to go, and go immediately.

So they are now with Bob and Alice Charnley. There is a funny feeling of liberation developing inside Judy. It is too soon yet for her to feel really safe, but already she is feeling that things are **new** and somehow, **clean.** Judy would not use these words about feelings. She does not put them into words, these feelings, but if you have worked a long time with children whose souls have been enslaved, you can tell when they are being liberated.

Judy is still somewhat confused, but not as confused as she was at home or with the Burrows. At first with Bob and Alice it was even worse than when she first went to the Burrows. Then, at least, she **thought** she knew what to do, but this time she cannot use even the ploys she had learnt at home — so what **do** people do to get loved and wanted, and to belong? The strangest thing of all is that you do not have to engage in any 'secret' games in order to make 'Uncle Bob' like you — he just likes you. He also goes along with Alice in showing you how to live and what to do. And if you make a mistake, he and Alice both tell you the same thing about how to do things. Nobody asks a price for anything.

Judy still feels pain about her parents. But the worst pain she feels is when she thinks about — Robo. **Robo** was a little dog her dad brought her 'For being a good girl in a secret'. Until she came to Bob and Alice Charnley (and she's still not quite sure of them) **Robo** was the only person, well **animal** if you like, who gave her love without asking for something ------ something nasty.

Tony is still fairly aggressive. He still draws pictures about people being cruel to other people or to animals. He still wets his bed and often wakes in the night screaming. He has drawn pictures of his dreams. There is always lots of sick about, and sometimes cut-up bodies. When he came into care there were lots of bruises all over Tony's body. There were weals around his wrists and ankles where he had been bound screaming to the bed or to other pieces of furniture. Tony screamed but he did not actually cry. Screaming eased the pain. Then the hands that should have cared for him prized open his buttocks and his Dad's 'willie' went up his bottom. His bottom was sore and he soiled his pants a lot.

Tony knew that Judy had to do 'secrets'. She had told him — only him, no-one else. But why was it that she was kissed and petted in her 'secrets' whilst he was beaten and bruised?

'Tony always recoils when you go to put your arm round him' said Alice Charnley recently. In fact, I've seen him put his hands up and wince when I've only intended to put my hand on his shoulder. Bodies touching spark off a mixture of sensations in Tony. At the Burrows, before people found out about 'secrets', Tony found that he felt strong and powerful if he could do to other children's bodies what had been done to his body — and that was where power came from. It will take a long time for Tony to heal. Fortunately, no-one will be asking a price for offering friendship and affection. Perhaps in another year's time Bob and Alice, or one of them, will be able to place an arm round his shoulder. It could be a race against time, perhaps he will be 'in trouble' with the law before he can heal sufficiently. In that case he will sink into a mire of emotional and social degradation.

Clive

'What sort of a mind has this child got?' queried a frustrated teacher. 'He's capable of doing work above the average for his school year and yet he'll stand there and tell you a cock and bull story — a complete lie — when surely, he must have the nous to know that anyone can see through it. If you fished him out of the canal dripping wet, he'd stand there and tell you he'd never been near it!'

'And boast -----' continued Clive's teacher 'some of the claims he makes are impossible! Well, highly improbable. Whatever the subject under discussion Clive manages to work the conversation round to an account of his prowess or his family riches or his fantastic experiences. He **has** to be one up on the others all the time. He can just manage three lengths in the swimming pool now, but of course **he** was able to swim, so he says, at six days old! He had all his classmates incredulous with a tale of how, at six days old, his mother chucked him in at the deep end and he swam two lengths!'

Clive is ten years old, and like many of the disturbed and deprived children we are describing, he finds the school setting to be anything but conducive to conforming habits. As for his thought process, his 'mind' as the teacher put it, this is baffling to most people. Some bits of the process seem to be brilliant whilst other bits seem to be stuck, or not to be there at all. He seems rather like a half-put-together jigsaw puzzle, there are lots of unexpected spaces.

One very large space in this jigsaw puzzle is waiting for the bit called **Conscience.** Clive doesn't appear to have any. Although he may violently denounce anyone, child or adult, whom he feels has belittled him, or cheated him he shows no sorrow nor repentance, and certainly not remorse, when he has been shown up as a thief who has stolen from those who want to love and care for him. He has been known to damage the reputation of loving adults whose feelings have been terribly hurt as a result of the fibs he told, yet he seems incapable of **feeling** regret or sorrow, although he will readily say 'sorry'.

Another space in the jigsaw puzzle is awaiting the bit which has to do with understanding about **time** and **space.** For some reason, although Clive is capable of doing a fairly stiff crossword puzzle intended for adults, he has a blind spot when it comes to thinking about time. He even gets the week mixed up and will suddenly assume on Wednesday that the next day is Sunday.

Clive wets his bed at least four times a week and is sometimes doubly incontinent so that soiled underpants are not uncommon, not that he would bother overmuch, because discomfort, and even pain, doesn't seem to affect him unless very severe.

Because of Clive's 'problems' at school there are often dramatic scenes involving teachers and 'dinner ladies'. Clive usually resorts to extremely foul and abusive language on these occasions. He frequently locks himself in the lavatories and has been known to refuse to come down from the roof of some building whilst hurling four letter words of abuse and obscenity at the staff. Once or twice a month he is carried home, legs flaying, by the school caretaker because they've 'had enough of him' for one day.

The reader would be forgiven for forming a picture of this child's physical appearance in accordance with the description I have given so far of his personality — that is to say a rather objectionable, unpleasant looking specimen of childhood. In reality, however, he is a most appealing child to look at, with widely spaced large blue eyes and an alabaster forehead. He has a winning smile and a most ingratiating manner with people, especially strangers. As a little child he was extremely pretty. Furthermore, he can be an engaging and entertaining companion.

Clive does not believe in permanency, nor does he feel secure about constancy. 'Shifting Sands' would best describe his experience of life so far, and this expression may be applied as much to his **feelings** about human relationships and social behaviour as to his actual belongingness and the different 'families' he has experienced.

Nothing **belongs** to Clive except his own body and his own thoughts. Yet, although the 'shifting sands' feeling is always there, he must not let other people, children or adults, know about this.

Other children often use the possessive (plural) adjective to describe things which they have. They talk about **'Our** car' and **'Our** house' and **'Our** caravan' or holiday bungalow, as if these things are held in joint ownership with their parents. Clive, who has had eleven moves, not counting hospitalization and the times he has run away, has found a way of possessing or sharing ownership so that he too can talk like that about 'Our' possessions — and go several claims further! He simply (without any conscience) appropriates the best articles from the many 'placements' he has experienced and produces a collection of 'our' things which surpasses those of the other kids. He takes a superb garden from one 'Home' or a family he has lived with, some beautiful and extravagantly expensive paintings from another; a flashy sports car from a third, and so on. These become what 'our' dad or 'our' uncle and aunt share with him. Clive feels good, he feel safe, he feels the same, only better than them, when he describes what 'we' have. He is 'boasting and fantasising' again!

The safe or good feelings do not last long with Clive. The dispossessed — 'Not as good as them' feelings quickly return, especially when people challenge and examine and destroy his fantasy and 'boasting' talk unmercifully.

Clive is a competitive child, compulsively so. Competition is not something pleasant for him. Competition represents the struggle for an acceptable identity. His is a thirsty, devouring, compulsive personality; thirsty for recognition, unable to share affection, although unable as yet to invest anything approaching a purity of affection in anyone else.

Clive is in a residential centre for children. He competes avidly with all the other children in the centre. Not in the way people think of when they fondly talk of competition being 'good' for society — he competes for belongingness and attention. Clive burns up with a jealous, angry feeling if another child is sitting next to any member of staff. He will attempt to disrupt any quiet scene in which perhaps another child is enjoying an 'arm round the shoulder cuddle-up' while watching T.V. He may try to squeeze in between the child and adult, or squash up on the other side of the adult. He cannot bear attention or affection going in any other direction but towards himself.

It is the same with conversation. Clive must monopolise it, and as he has a good vocabulary and is an intelligent, lively child, he succeeds unless controlled. But he misinterprets control and experiences it as rejection.

Despite the traits I have already described, this child is able to present himself as a different person to different people. He has an uncanny gift of perceiving the likes and dislikes, strengths and weaknesses, abilities and failings of adults and children, so that he can be to one and all, the child who is in tune with each. He knows just which button to press! In the early days of his time at the children's centre, therefore, it was difficult to be certain that you were talking about the same child, and written reports were contradictory.

In the end, of course, this chameleon-like behaviour leads to impossible situations. Clive then moves into his panic stage, his running-away-from-it-all stage, and he does 'run' ------ he is an 'absconder'. When he is missing Clive usually 'sleeps rough'. He feels free! Free from the agony of being --- who? Which image? Free from compulsive competition. **And,** what is more, he is **punishing** 'them'. He often gets caught shop-lifting on these runs.

Vivien

She is eleven and a half years old, and just before she was taken into care at ten years old, she wrote the letter (overleaf) to her stepmother and natural father.

Vivien's early life had been lived as the sixth child of a family, or should we say a **household,** of eight children. The two siblings immediately above her shared the same father. There were two other fathers somewhere in the picture to account for all eight children.

Vivien has memories of being left in the house with her two younger brothers and an older sister, when she herself was five and Marion, the sister, was six and a half. She remembers that when anyone knocked at the door, all four children hid under the table, as they'd been told to do.

She remembers her natural mother as a large, cuddly woman with a particular and very special mummy smell. Sometimes when passing a rather ripe garbage bin on a warm day she experiences special

D~~ea~~r ~~Mum~~ Step muther and Dad
I am runin away from here becors yous orl hate me anyhow I hate yous to and I am fed up with yous getting at me and me ge ting locked in me room and getting me bum hit and any way I will tell the polis of yous

Orl yous cares a bowt is our Mavis and your Jakeline and our Peter and I am fed up with orl yor rows and shoutin and you nickt my post hoffice bank books muny

Do not look for me

I hates yous forever

Vivien

smells which somehow bring back a 'long-time-ago' feeling.

Adults who have known the family for some years would give you a different, grown-up, outsider, account of the family as it was when Vivien was five. They would describe Dorothy Webster, Vivien's mother, as an extremely fat, slobbering, 'fish wife' of a woman who spent as much time in the local psychiatric ward as she did at home. That would account for all the strange exaggerated stories Vivien tells about fabulously rich people in her past life, and living in a 'big rich house' — these were various fostering and residential care experiences.

Some of these adults would tell you what a filthy state the home was usually in, and the rich smell of urine and stale beds and ------ garbage? — that greeted you.

We need not be concerned here with the details of the intervening years between five and ten. For long periods Vivien was in care.

When not in care she bounced about between 'home' with Mum and whoever else happened to be there, and various reluctant relatives or 'mates' of mum. At nine years of age the Social Services Department discharged her to the care of her natural father now that he was married and 'settled down'.

From the day she was discharged to the care of her father and step-mother Vivien **punished** everyone in sight. That's my word — **punished.** So far as Vivien was concerned she was getting her own back on whoever was 'mean' or nasty to her, which meant most people, but especially teachers, social workers, and anyone in authority.

Vivien has recently changed her image so far as physical appearance is concerned. She has started to take an interest in her hair and to ask for in-fashion girl's clothes. Until recently she eschewed such things and went about looking as wild and uncouth as she could.

'Nobody would believe what she does' said her foster mother recently. And indeed, looking at this child, who in her school uniform looks so conforming and as pleasant a girl as you'd meet, few people **would** believe what she does. Stealing money from home (i.e. the foster home) or secretly consuming a box of birthday chocolates belonging to the foster mother's daughter is of course commonplace and such bits of behaviour are frequently met with, but urinating in the family coffee mugs is something more special — so is tying the cat's front and back paws together and chucking it into the next door garden. 'Pretty child' said a colleague of mine when I showed her a photo of Vivien!

As is my usual practice, before meeting Vivien for the first time I tried to get a picture of how other people had felt about her. There were some comments which, with slight variations, occurred frequently:

> 'Vivien never looks you in the eye'
> 'She gives people a terrible look — sort of half closes her eyes — a real dirty look it is!'
> 'Other children's parents are always complaining about her attacking their kids'

But not all the comments are critical of Vivien's behaviour or moods:

> 'She sings when she's happy'

'I can't understand it, she's lovely sometimes with little kids, especially babies'

'She knows how to enjoy herself though. She's marvellous at sport and she really lets herself go at swimming, roller skating, dancing, pop-music and all that'

'Well, yes, she has got a sense of humour but it's what I call **banana skin** humour — she likes slap-stick stuff'

Some of the comments made about Vivien reflect the way certain of the adults in her life have thought and acted. As I got to know her it became clear that some of the ideas held about her were what people **wanted** to see in her, rather than what actually existed. Sometimes it was possible to trace the effect of adult intrigues. Take this statement as an example. It was written into the child's case file as a comment made by her father:

'She hasn't seen her own mother for three years ------ she doesn't want to either'.

The first part was true. Everyone had colluded to keep all thought, all discussion, all memory of 'Mum', big slobbery (or soft, cuddly'?) mum, out of Vivien's life. And the longer this went on, the more beautiful in the child's mind became her mother, and the more warm, cosy, and comforting became that smelly, squalid house. The second part of the father's statement, the part the social workers and foster parents had been working to '------ she doesn't want to either' was not true.

An exasperated teacher said to me. 'Somebody needs to be able to get right inside her to find out what's going on'. Some of the exasperation was generated by Vivien's disruptive behaviour in class, some by the contradictory and ironic behaviour she displays in her relationships with other people.

Like other young adolescents Vivien has 'crushes'. But if you have a crush on someone why annoy and irritate and embarrass them? Why **punish** them? Why spray-can all over the school wall 'Mr. Donaldson — Vivien — Fuck'?

Vivien seldom cries. for about six years now she's hardly shed a tear — at least so far as I or anyone else in touch with her knows. She might cry to herself, perhaps when she's alone in bed. You would have thought that a girl who had gone through all her life-disrupting experiences would have cried and cried. There was a time when she used to cry easily. That was when she **felt** love.

It was on those occasions when she had suddenly, mysteriously, to leave the place where she felt love and go somewhere else, that she'd cried — because of that love feeling. When she was little and someone said her mother (her 'real' mother) was coming to see her, and when she'd waited, looking out of a window, and her mother did not come — that was when she had cried at first. Perhaps she had cried because she had **felt** a kind of love again. Gradually she did not feel love when nasty things happened. Gradually the feeling she got when her mother did not turn up was a different feeling that burnt her inside. Gradually she did not want the love feeling nor the burnt up feeling — she wanted **no** feeling. She stopped crying.

Now she seldom cries. Of course not, how can strong, tough, 'couldn't care less' kids who know how to fight, and who say they'll 'demolish yer face!' be seen crying. Besides, what about the gang at school — her mates — the ones who rely on her to get the teachers all stewed up? Strictly speaking it will have to be a new gang now because Vivien has just got 'suspended' from school again. It's the teacher's fault of course — 'I hate Miss Harrison — I'll **do** 'er, I'll get locked up for 'er'

When people, including children, say they 'can't understand' Vivien, they may mean they are non-plussed by her behaviour —- usually it is adults who refer to her in that way. But they **may** mean that they quite literally cannot understand her language, for she is either sullen and morose, or highly excited, laughing loudly, shouting at the teachers and talking so rapidly in a strong northern accent that people literally cannot understand her. You can imagine the mileage some of the other kids get out of that:

> 'What's she on about? She can't even talk English — What you speakin, — Dutch?'
> 'Sh'd up yslf yer bldy woolerback'
> (Shut up yourself you bloody woolyback)
> 'Where d'you come from --- speaking' like that?'
> Yer just a snob — I hate snobs — gt lst (get lost) or 'll dermolish yer face'

Maybe this started off as one more attempt by one more child of Vivien's peer group to make friends with her. Of course the other girl shied off and agreed with the general viewpoint that Vivien is rough and aggressive and a trouble-maker. All of which is true.

Only Vivien knows about the **feelings.** The feelings speak to her.

They speak from inside her. They are another self inside her. The other self speaks to itself. It says 'I'm rubbish ------ Miss Harrison wants me to be in the school play and I'd like to but I'm rubbish --- I can't even talk English — I'll get laughed at - - I'll ruin her bloody old play — on purpose — then I'll get kicked out of the drama group — shit the drama group'.

And in Vivien's school report it says:

'Could be good at drama, and likes it, but deliberately disrupts the class and so is excluded from this year's production'.

Paul

Paul was adopted at the age of five and a half years, and I met him for the first time when he was six and a half. For Paul the world is like a constantly changing kaleidoscope. New colours, new shapes, new challenges occur every few minutes. Paul is exhaustingly interested in all the shapes, patterns, sounds and relationships, but he is also dramatically frustrated because he cannot do the things he should be able to do. Yet he dives into activities all the time, always ready to have a go. As soon as he finds he can't manage a task (i.e. within three or four minutes of starting the attempt) he throws it aside and **rushes** on to do something else. He's been **rushing** all his life and yet, as they say, he's getting nowhere fast.

Paul has been called 'clumsy', 'all thumbs', 'stupid' and quite a few other adjectives. He finds the world is a very frustrating place despite all the things of interest which abound. The children of his own age don't seem to exert themselves half as much as he does, yet they can throw balls up in the air and catch them as they come down — they can skip, which he finds is an impossible function even though he rushes to get hold of the skipping rope before anyone else.

And now grown-ups have started to restrict the things — ordinary things — he is **allowed** to do, whilst other children even younger than he, are allowed to do such things:

'I'll pour the milk out'
'No, Paul, leave it, let Jason do it, you'll spill it all'
'I'll unscrew the orange juice bottle'
'No, Paul, you'll knock the bottle over again'
'Please Mum, I'll open the boot for you'
'No, Paul, you'd better let me do it'

Paul has tried doing things quickly — in fact he's now got into the habit of trying to do things very quickly — partly to defeat any adult who may say 'No, Paul -----' and partly because he feels things should be done quickly since doing things at an 'ordinary' speed feels like doing them very slowly. To make matters worse, when Paul does things at **his** speed he invariably fails at the task, whatever it is, simply because of the ridiculous speed.

Living with Paul is a strenuous activity in itself. His day begins at 5.30 a.m. when he may feel inclined to leap out of bed and rush round the house, or play with the dog, who incidentally feels that Paul is the best thing that has happened since dog- biscuits. In fact his adoptive parents (referred to in the future as parents) have got him to the stage where he is able to remain in bed until 6.30 a.m. engaged in about ten different play activities, including crayoning, motor-cars, aeroplanes and a bed-side video show.

Halfway through dressing, he forgets about the function and is found examining the inside of a broken toy. Ablutions are hectic and it is difficult to know why the taps in the bathroom shoot upwards, towards the ceiling when Paul is washing.

During breakfast, the whole energetic, active, non-stop machine chatters away, knocks things over, rushes to crack open his egg or cut into his scrambled egg on toast before an adult pounces and does it for him. His speed results in the food shooting off the plate on to the floor. The day proceeds in this manner, and at this speed.

In these descriptions of children I am avoiding giving labels to their behavioural characteristics, but there is no doubt about it, two characteristics stand out as far as Paul is concerned. One, he is abnormally active — we could say overactive — and two, he is able to spend only a very short time with any activity.

These two characteristics on their own are enough to run him into all sorts of trouble and problems at school, but he has other ingredients just to enrich the mixture. It seems difficult, if not impossible, for Paul to work on his own in an ordinary non- special class. He wants to **do** things on his own (for five minutes flat that is) but not necessarily the things the other children are doing, but he also wants his teacher to sit next to him, otherwise he wanders about the classroom, 'interferes' with other children's work and is generally 'disruptive'.

Once again, he **knows** what he wants to do and is aware that other children can do certain things which he feels he should do. In fact he feels that **this** time he **will** be able to do it. So he tags onto some group game in the playground, some game involving skills such as skipping or ball catching or kicking. Once again he fuddles the whole thing and then;

'Get out of it Paul Hopkins, you're rubbish, you're not in the game'
'Yes I am ----- it's my ball anyway, so there'
'No you're not, get out of it — we don't need your ball anyway 'cause Richard's got a ball — so shuv off'

Paul shuvs off. Feelings come up inside him. The same feelings he used to have when he was living with Marlene. He always refers to his natural mother, whom he remembers, as 'Marlene'. Paul's life with Marlene is another story altogether, but it connects up with the Paul of today. That word the kids used when they turned him out of the game ('Rubbish') that was what Marlene had said over and over again '-----rubbish, you're rubbish — can't even hold a spoon — and sit down will you ----- I said **sit** down - --- God! Why did I get you?'

Paul did not lose confidence in himself as many children would have done. He never got the feeling that he was rubbish because **he** couldn't do certain things, he just went right on rushing in to do it next time. Perhaps he lacked some sensitivity? Perhaps he ought to have felt 'I'm rubbish --- I can't do these things' - but he didn't. The feelings that came up inside him were hateful, unfair feelings. People were unfair.

There were some feelings Paul did not experience. He did not experience the feeling that he was **special** to anyone, not even to Marlene. He tried to feel special to her but the feeling kept being brushed away. Gradually he developed a feeling of freedom if Marlene kept away and didn't touch him. Gradually he wanted to be a butterfly or a bird and not be tied to anyone or anything.

Talking about being 'tied' to things, Paul has experienced this literally when he lived with Marlene — she dealt with his overactiviity by tying him to his bed. He still has a scar where the rope bit into his wrist. Paul gradually developed another feeling, or perhaps it was a kind of intuition, which said 'Don't be tied to anybody — keep a distance between you and people, even though you want their attention'.

This feeling, this intuition, made for a bit of a problem some months after Paul had been placed for adoption. He was beginning to lose this feeling, but it was still there so he had to be careful. Being careful — Paul didn't actually **think** in those terms, or use those words, he only **felt** — but being careful meant trying it out with **one** person at first. He just let one person get close — not too close but a bit closer. He sat on his mother's lap and insisted that only she could tell him his bed- time story, and only she could bath him. His father began to feel rejected and left out by this little boy who at first had allowed him to play with him and bath him. Paul could not cope with making close relationships with more than one person at that stage. Although he didn't realize it, he was healing. It was hard for the adults to appreciate this. Even 'normal' adults can easily feel left out, not wanted, and hurt.

* * * * *

So there are my eleven children. I have introduced them to you at a time in their lives when they are all needing a fair amount of help and understanding.

In some instances I have given you a small amount of the background or history concerning the child, and no doubt this has helped you to see that (to coin a phrase) there is more in it than meets the eye, but I have not attempted to look closely at the processes (social and psychological as well as physical) which affected these children over the years of their growth. I hope to do that in the rest of the book.

No doubt the reader will have picked out several experiences which some of the children had — but should not have had. I shall look more closely at these experiences in Chapter Three which I have called **Damaging lumber.** But as well as the experiences they should not have had, our children have **missed out** on many experiences which are vital for healthy physical and psychological development. I shall consider these missed-out experiences in the following chapter: **Lost riches.**

CHAPTER TWO

Lost Riches

What are these **lost riches?** The children I have described in chapter one had all missed-out on some very valuable, essential elements in their life experiences. I believe the things they missed out on were very often the most important things in life. So what are these things? Am I talking about 'riches' in material terms? **Things?** Maybe the cars or the computers? Cash or expensive toys? These are all **things,** and admittedly in introducing this chapter I have spoken of **things** they have missed out on.

Essentially however, it is not **things** at all I am thinking of. Some of these children have more material 'riches' than many much happier and more stable children. They and their parents, or foster parents, are rolling in wealth when compared with people from simpler societies, at least as far as goods and chattels, automobiles and hi-fi etc., are concerned. In the jargon of todays economics, they are doing well, many of them, so far as the 'standard of living' is concerned, but they have missed out earlier on **quality of life** rather than standard of living. Yes, some of them missed out on both, but I am going to argue that it was the missed-out precious experiences — the poor **quality** of life, that has left the scars in their personality development I have described in chapter one.

Without condemning their natural parents, for many of them suffered in the same way, it is true to say that the children I have described — or most of them — lost out on what we may call a good-enough parenting experience. I shall return to some of these terms later when we look more deeply into the experience of the children. For now I simply want to introduce the **non-things** aspects of nurture.

Of course, material needs such as food and warmth and safe, dry accommodation, and toys and baths and washing machines are all important, and have to be provided for children and their parents, but even if all that is taken care of, our children can grow up angry, unhappy, aggressive or withdrawn, and can move on to delinquency, neurosis, drug-dependency and the rest ---- why? How?

There are children who have never experienced good-enough parenting. There are others who were actually cherished by loving parents in their infancy, but, as a result of some tragedy, suffered **loss,** emotional loss as well as physical separation, through death or illness. There are others who seem actually to have experienced parental deprivation as a result of the 'care' system itself. They have moved about, sometimes like **parcels** rather than nomads, from 'placement' to 'placement' since they have been 'in care', — Stevey, for instance, with his three Children's Homes and six foster homes. In his case the local authority was acting as parent and guardian. One of the things about good-enough parenting is that the child is given the **continuity** of parent figures.

Two of the most important non-things in good-enough parenting are **Attachment** and **Bonding** of which I shall say something more later in this chapter. For now, I shall not be concerned with academic definitions although some psychologists place a lot of emphasis upon good-enough attachment. Let me just say in a simplistic manner that by attachment I mean the child's attraction towards and feeling of safety-belongingness to the parent, and by Bonding I mean the parent's attraction towards and feelings of protective-belongingness to the child.

If it will help, for the time being, you can think of two magnets (of opposite poles) attracting each other. Our children have sometimes missed out altogether on attachment and bonding, but quite often the attachment and bonding has been weak or faulty or mixed in with feelings of intense fear or hatred:

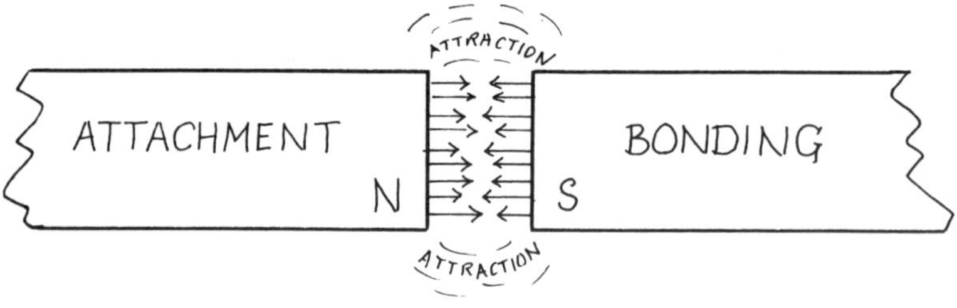

Later in this book we shall briefly consider the effects of failures in the attachment-bonding process but at this stage I simply want to emphasise an aspect which is not yet widely recognised. I want to emphasise the point that in the case of many children who are, or have been deprived of good-enough parenting, the effects may be seen in several elements of the child's personality.

In the descriptions of the children in chapter one the reader will have noticed that all sorts of behaviour and emotional problems abound. It is possible, by simplifying things a bit, to group these problems under such headings as **Social** and **Emotional.** By **Social** I mean the way the child behaves towards other people, how he interacts. So we can think of thirteen-year old Robert finding it more comfortable to play with little kids of seven or eight rather than mix with his own peer group. We can also think of Judy and the way she tried to interact with her foster father in a sexual way. These, and many, many other bits of behaviour can be categorised (in a simplistic categorisation admittedly) as **Social** behaviour or social interaction.

Under the heading of **Emotional** (or **Affective** to use a wider, more technical term) we could put the feelings (i.e. 'emotional feelings', in everyday language) of Judy's brother, Tony, who found that he 'felt strong and powerful if he could do to other children's bodies what had been done to his body'. Usually, however, there is an overlap between the emotional and the social and, unless a person tells us how they feel, we deduce their feelings from their behaviour — so, if we go back to Robert again, it is possible to see in him **some** bits of behaviour which are really quite typical of an eighteen-month or two-year old child but are viewed as peculiar, if not annoying in a thirteen- year old lad, such as when he 'jumps up and down, whoops loudly, claps his hands, or laughs in an exaggerated and 'silly' fashion' when something exciting or pleasing occurs, or when he 'clings' to his parents.

Children (and adults) can be emotionally retarded just as they may be intellectually retarded, but we tend not to excuse them in the same way. An emotionally 'stuck' ten-year-old may have the frequent temper-tantrums of the two-year-old, for example. Some older, deprived children, have a need to obtain emotional satisfaction in the way we assume a baby or infant experiences emotional satisfaction as a result of being held, cuddled, and in the case of Sally (chapter one) of being 'babied'. Being 'stuck' emotionally may also mean that strong negative feelings surge up if the child feels anyone else is competing for attention. The child Stevey found competition very difficult, and so did Clive with his 'thirsty, devouring, compulsive personality. Thirsty for recognition, unable to share affection - ----'

So, we can put some bits of behaviour, some of the unusual or problematic styles of development, under these headings of **Social** and **Emotional.** But deprived children are affected in other ways which may at first seem to have little to do with nurturing or parenting (or holding, cuddling, talking to, providing moral guidance, playing with etc.) and yet the retardation or unusual development in these areas may result from social and emotional deprivation. We can provide two more headings for problems in these areas of development. The two headings are **Physical** and **Cognitive** (understanding, knowing, thinking, reasoning etc.)

Under the heading **Physical** I would include examples of what we call poor **motor** development. By **motor** development we mean the child's ability to use her limbs and fingers, to use her body that is, in a co-ordinated way so that she is able to perform tasks which are in line with children of her own age group. Clearly, there are many children, most of them who have experienced good-enough parenting, who have physical and motor development problems which are not to do with deprivation, so you have to be very careful about making judgements here, and children who appear to have poor physical co-ordination or developmental problems should be seen by medical experts. Nevertheless it is becoming more widely recognised that some forms of physical retardation, including poor motor co-ordination, may result from or be associated with social and psychological deprivation.

Concerning the children I introduced to the reader, it will be recalled that several of them suffered as infants from a syndrome referred to medically as Non-organic Failure to Thrive. This applied to Sally, Michelle and John. Robert was 'dead clumsy' and just could not cope with the **fine** (finger) manipulation to light a match without danger. Paul ran into all sorts of trouble because he was so 'clumsy' and accident prone, and people called him 'all thumbs' and 'stupid'. He could not make objects do what he wanted them to do. In fact he found it hard to make his body do the things other kids could do. He could not catch balls and he could not skip. Yet there was 'nothing wrong' with Paul so far as his brain and nervous system and limbs were concerned. This retardation in **his** case was something to do with his whole life experience, especially his infant care.

Still more astonishing, perhaps, is the connection which appears to exist between good-enough parenting and the ability to reason or understand. I am not saying that these children are adversely affected to the extent that a truly learning-difficulty or brain damaged child may be affected. Indeed many of the children I refer to are as sharp as needles in much of their thinking and understanding. So much so that they are liable to be labelled **crafty** or **cunning** (and they have often learnt to survive by such means). But although some of these kids are quite smart in much of their thinking, there are often areas which don't seem to function, at least not in line with the average child of a similar age.

Such children sometimes find it hard to grasp concepts (or ideas) which have to do with **time** and **space** (e.g. distance, shape). Some seem to have problems over **cause and effect.** I often meet foster parents or parents who feel that a child is being stubborn or 'not trying' when they do not seem to understand about the meaning of terms like 'two weeks' or they still cannot tell the time at eight or nine years of age when they can 'understand' all about money or computers! Clive (chapter one) was like this and he couldn't sort out the days of the week.

So, let us bear in mind that poor parenting, poor nurture during the early months and years of life, and continuing emotional privation over the following years, may result in the person being adversely affected in one or more aspects of personality; in one or more of the **developmental modes.**

It may help some readers if we use the analogy of 'white' light going through a prism and coming out the other side broken up into its rainbow colours. If you can imagine that we could beam a child's character or personality through a prism and see it coming out the other side broken up into these developmental modes, it would look something like this:-

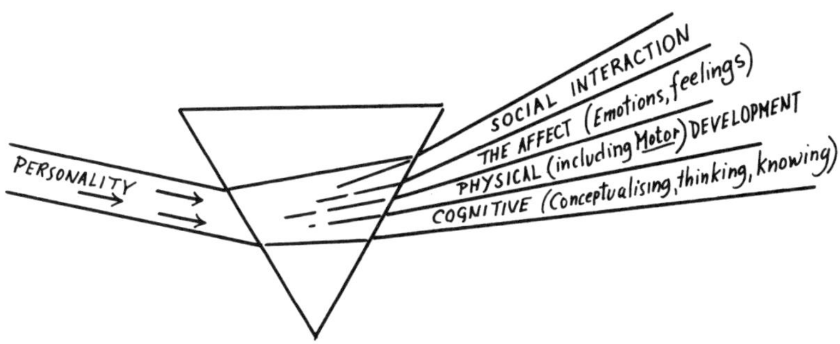

These four developmental modes cannot in reality be separated in this way or even studied in isolation, but I hope that by thinking about them in the way we have done, we shall remember that the deprived child may be affected in all these aspects of personality and development. The whole person, or any aspect of the person, may be injured by poor nurturing and by abusive treatment, not only the emotional bit.

Missing experiences

Since I am talking about **lost riches** in this chapter, and because I have already indicated that I do not mean just material wealth, but the right kind of **experiences,** it may be helpful if we spend a little time considering these experiences. Again, in order to help us to look at children's needs and the missing (or previously missed-out) experiences, I am putting them into two slightly artificial groups. So I want to talk about **Emotional (Affective)** experiences and **Sensory** experiences.

By affective experiences I mean all the experiences a child (or adult) has and which cause him or her to have those inner (soul!) feelings about being loved or being wanted, or about feeling safe or feeling left out, or shy, or jealous or angry. By sensory experiences I mean those experiences concerned directly with the five senses of **touch, sight, hearing, smell,** and **taste** (the last two certainly merge in together).

If children are brought up in a way which provides the right kind of affective and sensory experiences together with care-givers (parents, siblings etc.) who can help to interpret and make use of these experiences, then we may say that the children had certain **riches** in their lives. If, as will be the case with the children I have introduced to the reader in chapter one, they have missed out on these experiences, then we can understand what is meant by the title of this chapter — **Lost riches.**

John Triseliotis has rightly said that concepts such as identity, security and sense of belonging are difficult to define or measure (1983) but nevertheless I am sure that we can have a meaningful discussion about disturbed and deprived children and how best to help them even if we are forced to use rather everyday and imprecise words. I would like now to consider in a little more detail what I mean by **lost riches** thinking first about the importance of affective experiences.

The little girl, Michelle, I described in chapter one, missed-out on what Triseliotis (1983) referred to as a 'sense of belonging'. I wrote this about Michelle:

> There was something bad about people who were there at one time, being warm and cuddling you, or even shouting at you but still being there, and then **not** being there. There was something frightening about these people because they had something to do with this 'don't want you anymore' feeling.

The reader will also recall Clive's feelings about human relationships and how these reflected his feelings about permanency. 'Shifting sands', I said would best describe his experience of life so far. Nothing belonged to Clive and Clive did not belong anywhere or to anyone — so far as his feelings were concerned.

Triseliotis (1983) has said:

> '... it is not possible for a person to develop a secure identity if he does not experience a sense of belonging within a secure family and social environment. '

In the article from which I have quoted, Triseliotis is drawing from a larger study which 'contrasted people who grew up adopted, with people who grew up in long-term fostering — average 11 years with the same foster parents' He goes on to say:

> 'About half of the respondents in each of the two groups spoke with real enthusiasm and satisfaction about their growing up experiences and the quality of care they received by their adoptive or foster families. Both groups indicated that strong feelings of attachment and psychological bonds developed between themselves and their 'substitute' parents. These close relationships continued into adult life and were a source of continued mutual satisfaction and support. These respondents felt secure, wanted and loved by their 'parents' and **experienced a strong sense of 'belonging' (my emphasis).**

The ingredients in parenting and nurturing generally, which produce this 'sense of belonging' are in fact some of the 'riches' I have referred to. So often are they taken for granted that we do not think about them as riches, and certainly not as wealth. yet without these ingredients children grow up with impoverished lives.

The reader will have noticed that when describing the children I occasionally took liberties with the English language and coined words such as **belongingness** to describe feelings and experiences. Another word I use to describe one of the rich experiences in childhood is **specialness.** This is another quality so hard to define and to measure but the experience is real enough. Your own mother may like many other children, she may be a teacher and have a lot to do with other children. She may adore your child cousins and find the children who live next door attractive but you, as one of **her** children, feel **special.** You feel that you **are** special to her. Children enjoy the warm feeling of **specialness** to their parents and siblings, and usually to other family members such as grand-parents. Many of the children we are thinking about have missed-out on the **specialness** feeling.

Attachment

I have briefly introduced the concepts of attachment and bonding. Research workers have been interested in the question: what factors induce children to attach to particular people? Professor Schaffer (1985) writes:

> 'The notion that the first attachment emerges in physical care situations and is directed at whoever is responsible for the alleviation of hunger and pain and other such tension has not been born out: children may become attached to individuals who have never played any part in their physical care'.

Obviously the physical care of the child is extremely important, but in good-enough parenting there must be other ingredients which can't be measured so easily. A child can in fact come to feel the greatest security and warmth and belongingness to someone who is not the main feeder and nappy-changer and bather. Fortunately most parents are able to provide the physical care **and** these other ingredients, but in the case of our chapter one children they missed-out on them.

Schaffer, in the article quoted above, goes on to say:

> '---- a parental quality that does appear to play an important part in eliciting attachments is one that we might best refer to as **'sensitive responsiveness'**.' (my emphasis).

You could describe **sensitive responsiveness** as being 'in tune' with the child. Good-enough parents, and other members of a child's family, usually have enough sensitive responsiveness to ensure a happy enough attachment experience. In the case of newborn babies and young infants the signals given out by the child are **received,** where sensitive responsiveness exists, by the caregiver and correctly interpreted, and correctly responded to. Before long the caregiver is giving out signals (maybe by voice sounds, maybe by facial expression, etc.) and the child is interpreting.

By saying **sensitive** responsiveness, not just any kind of responsiveness, we mean an understanding and well-disposed responsiveness. the child, to put it in everyday language, **feels** that the concern, and love, and warmth are there. Yes, of course, good-enough parents sometimes misinterpret or they're tired or irritated by something and fail occasionally to respond in a **sensitive** way. And yes, as children grow older being 'in tune' with the child will include a sensitivity about how to control or correct him, and the child may not always 'like' it, but as we shall see shortly, as time goes on the child will develop a feeling of **Trust** concerning the parents and family, and life in general.

On the other hand, many of our children — those I have described - have often recoiled and turned away from the 'parent figures' or have become angry and frustrated as a result of their infant signals failing to be picked up, or because their 'parent figures' were so out of tune with their basic needs. I can think of one baby girl I met, a child of about fifteen months, who had become apathetic and depressed but was described as 'destructive' because she picked bits off her plastic pram. This child could not walk, or play. She would have done so, but her totally out of tune parents had kept her without any toys or objects of amusement (or discovery), and always strapped her in a pram, or a cot, or a high chair. **Sensitive** responsiveness is another of the **riches** these children have missed or lost. Sensitive responsiveness may be weak even in well to do families where children are surrounded by material wealth, but where no-one is really in tune with the child's essential feeling and belongingness needs.

Sensory experience

It is easier, perhaps, to attribute damage to the child's personality development resulting from the missed-out affective experiences.

But life experience does not come in bits all separate like a jigsaw puzzle. On the one hand we have to think about the **wholeness** of the child's experience, (he doesn't analyse and split experiences up as I'm doing in this book), and on the other hand we must think of the child as a whole. He experiences life. He touches things; tastes things; smells, hears and sees objects. But at the same time he **learns** about shape, size, hardness, softness, and so on. And, again at the same time, he will be associating learned attitudes with various objects ('nasty' 'nice' 'big' etc.)

Gradually, the way he responds to objects (including humans in this case) will be understood by him as 'good' or 'bad', 'safe' or 'dangerous'. The whole life experience is bound up in one package, so to speak, and this means that many of the early **sensory** experiences are linked into affective experiences for the young child. This linkage stays with us, sometimes in our unconscious mind, throughout our lives.

We may not appreciate what 'riches' children are experiencing for example, when they are paddling in streams and building dams with stones amongst the boulders, or when they are digging in sand, or petting their animals, or riding on an adult's shoulder; romping, or walking through dry fallen leaves which rustle as they kick their way through them.

Actually, come to think of it, even the way our society or culture is structured may provide or deprive children in terms of sensory experience. Rocking-cots are now seen only in folk museums or old pictures, and some quite intelligent parents have been surprised at the effect of gently rocking and **singing** their baby to sleep after almost despairing about the wakefulness of the child. The baby girl I mentioned above missed-out on these affective and sensory experiences.

We are finding, in our work with deprived and disturbed children, that some of them need to be given a form of treatment which has been referred to as 're-alerting the senses'. (Redgrave 1987). Either through deprivation or shock there is a sensory dullness or misinterpretation, or a desire (which could be described as a **hunger**) for stimulation of one or more of the senses. When I first started my work with children I came across many five- and six-year olds who had been brought up in big impersonal institutions — forty or more children being 'cared for' by one adult. Some of these children would crowd round and **touch** me or actually stroke my arm and **feel** the material of my jacket.

Talking of touch, Ashley Montague (1971) suggests that the human infant has a need to be touched 'and stroked' if development is to be satisfactory. In Europe and America there is a lot of proper concern at present on account of child sexual abuse and 'wrong' touching. There is a danger, however, of swinging so far in the 'safe' direction that caregivers become afraid of touch in any form and children become untouchables. According to Ashley Montague, children who have experienced satisfactory cuddling and holding will more likely develop sexually in a normal way.

I shall return in this chapter, to some further consideration of the missed-out sensory 'riches', and the loss of sensory enjoyment and exploration. Before discussing sensory experiential loss, however, I want to look again at the lost riches so far as inner feelings are concerned.

How does it feel?

There are many aspects of life which seem to be taken for granted by children who have not suffered prolonged deprivation or abuse, but which become nagging doubts or which generate feelings of smouldering 'anger' in children who have experienced prolonged abuse, rejection or constant moves from 'placement' to 'placement'.

I have simplified these complex feelings down to three basic questions. These questions are only occasionally verbalised by children, but they are often **felt.** They are:

Who am I?
Who do I belong with?
What will my future be?

I shall refer back to these questions, these feelings, now and again, because they are usually linked to the child's affective experience. They become **part of** the child's affective experience. They are associated with or generate feelings of doubt, confusion, apprehension, anger and so on.

We must use a lot of imagination and what is called empathy in order to put ourselves into the life experiences of these children. I have noticed, with cohesive families experiencing continuity, 'togetherness' and good-enough parenting that when the family comes together – which it does frequently for meals, pastimes or some sort of break, the members begin to enjoy **remembered,** shared life-experiences, often laughing together at the 'funny' bits!

'D'you remember when we were all in Sainsbury's and dad picked up a can of beans and a great big pile of cans — a whole big mountain of them — fell down and rolled all over the shop!?'

Or they might share sad-happy memories:

'I wish Auntie Louise was still alive'
'So do I'
'I've still got that picture she made for me — I love it'
'She didn't just make it for you, did she Mum?'
'Well, no, I think she meant to make you one each but she became too ill, so she said she'd like you all to share it'
'You can't remember Auntie Louise can you? You're too young'
'But I put flowers on my auntie Loozes gwave, I did'

These shared memories are more important than people realise, and I find that when adults come together, people who were children together or have experienced life together as adults, they love to relive the past.

Try to put yourself in the position of a ten or twelve year old who has been moving on from placement to placement and who has some pleasant memories of 'a long time ago' and some sad memories, but is in touch with **nobody,** and never likely to be in touch with anyone who was part of the scene belonging to those memories, nobody who can actually **share** the past.

'Who am I?' The child's roots, her past, her birth and what sort of welcome she had into the family, are part of the necessary ingredients to produce a taken for granted feeling — 'I'm just me' — which does not need to question at all. Bruno Bettelheim (1987) writes:

'The goal in raising ones child is to enable him, first, to discover **who** he wants to be, and then to become a person who can be satisfied with himself and his way of life.'

Associated with the 'Who am I?' question are the feelings children have about their self-worth. It is hard to name the many 'riches' which go to give a child an assured feeling of self- worth. So many of our deprived children carry very poor self-images, even though they may hide the fact behind an aggressive, macho stance. Think of Vivien (chapter one) 'Only Vivien knows about the **feelings.** The feelings speak to her. They speak from inside her.

They are another self inside her. The other self speaks to itself. It says 'I'm rubbish ------''

Remember Stevey: 'How does it feel when your mother makes you walk three yards behind her when out shopping and you are six years old?'

Triseliotis (1983) referring to his research work with the sort of children we are concerned with, used the expression **Personal identity** which embraces my own terms 'self-worth' and 'self- identity'. He said:

> 'By personal identity I mean the kind of consciousness we all carry about — 'who' we are and the kind of self-image we have of ourselves.'

He goes on to say:

> 'For the purpose of this article three areas were selected for study which are said to make a big contribution to identity building:
>
> (i) a childhood experience of feeling wanted and loved within a secure environment;
>
> (ii) Knowledge about one's background and personal history; and
>
> (iii) the experience of being perceived by others as a worthwhile person.'

These factors are usually taken for granted, they do not need to be spelt out. The secure child just feels wanted. Yet they are in fact priceless riches.

It is not only a matter of **telling** children that they are loved and valued. That may be included of course, but it is the richness of everyday life that has been missing with our child examples. Compare the child who comes home at the end of the school day grasping some drawing or object he's made at school, and whose parent or other caregiver receives him with a hug and who shows an interest in the drawing, and maybe has a special place where it can be exhibited for a time; compare that child's experience to the one who is received first and foremost with a harangue about the condition of his clothes, no hug, a dismissive 'what's that you've got? Oh yes, very nice, go up and get changed and be quick, I'm late for work — no I'm afraid you can't put it up there dear, daddy wouldn't like it — now off you go'. Imagine this as nearly always the way it is, not just on the occasional off day.

In another case perhaps the mother, already tired from a long day, does her best to provide the warmth of feeling, but dad never has any time either for the children or for her. There's always **something** to be done. The family never sit down and share meals together, or play games, or construct something. It is not necessary for the main adult caregivers to be always involved with the child. Siblings, and the family as a whole, will provide the growth enriching experience a child needs as long as the parental attitudes are right.

We must remember, when caring for 'older' children (eight, ten, twelve years or even older) who may 'dawdle' in the bathroom, ('she takes hours to wash herself'), or who may only play 'rough' games, or are 'destructive', that such children will often have a need, unexpressed and unrecognised, **to be washed** by an adult, and are not necessarily ready (yet) to be 'grown-up' and independent. They may have missed out on so much of that healthy parental touching as infants. And as for the 'rough' games, they may not have had imagination awakened in them to play those lovely imaginative games where you pretend you're on a boat (on the two arm-chairs pushed together!), and maybe nobody ever read them stories as toddlers nor as seven-year-olds. They may need a lot of this now, when they are much older!

In chapter three we shall consider the long-term effects resulting, not from these missed-out 'riches', but from experiences the child should not have had. Before looking again at the importance of early sensory experiences, however, I shall give a brief quote to emphasise the importance of (affective) **feeling** experiences in a child's life. Norma Symonds who wrote the books 'The Secret Rose' (1987) slipped from being an unhappy, left-out child of quarrelling (adoptive) parents, to being heavily sexually assaulted and, by thirteen years, finding a certain pleasure in being able to gratify men, and then on through to drug (heroin) dependency, and right on to a heavy involvement with black witchcraft. She survived, and recovered, but she writes:

> 'If my story demonstrates anything it is that childhood experiences may sow a minefield of unexploded bitter memories, which cripple our adult development, creating no-go areas we cannot deal with ourselves.'

Transitional objects

The importance of early sensory experience is now being given more emphasis in the teaching of child development. Shortly I shall pick out a number of statements made by certain experts in that subject, but before doing so I want to emphasise once again the fact that these experiences do not come along in separate, distinct boxes, so to speak. Often the sensory experiences are closely involved with the affective and cognitive. A good example of this is to be found in what Winnicott (1968) (1985) has called the **Transitional object** but which parents and children will know by far less sophisticated, but definitely more descriptive names; names in fact which have usually been invented by the child. I am referring to those strange objects little children insist on taking to bed with them. I can think of some (from children I have known) and these were referred to as 'My bye-bye' 'my ungot' 'goo-goo' 'goosey' and 'purdee'.

Winnicott describes the importance of the **transitional object** in helping the infant to move away from a purely or mainly subjective idea of reality towards the idea of a shared experience of reality. A young baby experiences objects, including people, and all the environment beyond herself, i.e. the bits of the environment she comes into contact with, and in the early stages there is just **self** (me) and other (people or things). But of course the baby has no words and presumably only feels or experiences this relationship. We are on fairly solid ground (although proof would be another matter) if we assume that a three-months-old baby does not have an idea (or knowledge) that other people experience objects, so her whole concept of existence must be very subjective. She must feel very much the centre of the universe — the centre of existence.

Somewhere along the line the infant must come to know that others have a separate experience of objects. This growing understanding involves a psychological separating from parental figures and becoming (in an understood way) a separate person. There will be a **transitional** (moving across to new awareness) stage and, according to Winnicott's hypothesis, the **transitional object** helps a child to cope with this growing understanding. The **transitional object** as well as being something physically comforting, may represent a person (eg. parent) and to some extent helps the child to handle a sort of 'loss' whilst at the same time moving across to a more independent state.

Winnicott writes:

> 'If we deprive the child of the transitional objects and disturb the established transitional phenomena, then the child has only one way out, which is a split in the personality ------' (1985)

Where is she stuck?

Sometimes, when a child has had relationship and self-identity problems along the way, she may remain 'stuck' insofar as the transitional stage is concerned, or she may use objects from an earlier stage of her life because, despite the pain she felt on account of rejection or her own lack of trust and feelings of guilt, there were also 'nice' experiences, fleeting times when a little of the security feelings crept in. In Robert's case this was so, and even though I have described him when he was thirteen years old the reader will note that he would still **play** with little toy motor-cars, making motor-car noises — not just collecting model cars, which is a more sophisticated past-time. I have known children like Robert who have used little toy motor- cars to stand for **people,** and make them injure one another. I have also found that many boys who have had a weak relationship with their father were able to latch on to motor-car talk as the only area of communication with dad! Remember, in child development, objects, things, sensory experiences may also closely relate to cognitive and emotional development.

Sensory experience and emotional development

The reader may well query my earlier descriptions of 'missing sensory experiences' and 're-alerting the senses', and rightly point out that, apart from children who were physically handicapped, these kids will have enjoyed all the physical senses. Yes, of course they have always been able to see, touch (feel) hear, and so forth, but this is where we need to link the physical sensory experience into the emotional and social aspects of life experience. The key word in the statement made (above) that '---- these kids will have enjoyed all the physical senses', is the word **enjoyed.** Even where children have actually been surrounded by physical stimulants, and have had freedom of movement, they may well have been made to feel 'bad' or may even have experienced guilt feelings if they handled objects or got themselves messy, but in any case many children have been denied such things as paints, crayons, paper, mud, glue, etc. and have often been restricted to one room, six stories up.

Sensory experience and the emotional and trust-building experiences start very early in life and are linked. Even the way in which a parent figure bottle-feeds (or breast-feeds) an infant will either provide or deny certain 'riches' which are hard to replace in life — although they can be replaced if someone works hard at it. In feeding, all the senses of taste, smell, touch, sight and even sound are involved. The lips are full of delicate sensory nerve endings.

I once placed a new-born baby in a short-term foster home awaiting placement with long-term adopters. This baby girl would normally have been in the short-term foster home for about eight weeks, awaiting medical clearance, etc. This was a 'new' foster home, and although the foster mother had proved herself a loving, warm, capable 'good-enough' mother to her own two children (about seven and nine years old) she had not previously fostered children. She adored babies but could have no more of her own.

This baby was moved after five weeks because the foster mother could not cope. During that five weeks the child was very unsettled and cried almost continually, or so it seemed to the family. I was constantly telephoned about some new worry to do with the baby's physical condition ('has she got ingrowing toe nails that are hurting?') and the mid-wife and health visitor provided all the expertise normally provided.

The adopters were warned that they were likely to experience this baby (their first) as a very unsettled baby. They never experienced a single disturbed night, apart from the usual short period of wakefulness for feeding and changing. The baby slept peacefully during the day, and all went well.

The short-term foster mother was able to say that she felt unable to go on as a foster mother for babies, and I agreed with her. She told me that she had felt quite unsettled emotionally when the baby was with her. She had 'held back' in enjoying the baby. She had literally held back on cuddling the baby up to her (or even holding her firmly) at any time, feeding time included, not because she disliked these feelings but because she could not bear the thought of **bonding** with the infant when she knew she would soon have to part with her. That baby was picking up signals as a result of her sensory experiences.

Even in the most basic human function of excretion the process will involve the ordinary physical sensory feelings of bowel and anal movements **and** with pleasureable (or otherwise) feelings of relief and comfort (or discomfort) and, later on, even with cognitive/affective aspects of pride — **'clever** girl, she's done do-dos for mummy'.

Unfortunately such basic processes may also become associated with feelings of guilt or rejection, or they may be used by the child to 'punish' or control. This may apply to feeding as well as elimination. In these examples we are restating the fact that the sensory, affective and cognitive modes of development are closely linked, Gaussen (1984) Richards (1974) Scaffer (1977) Buda et al (1972).

A large amount of a child's time should be spent in play. But let us briefly examine what it is we are talking about when we refer to **play.** Much of **play** is about learning the nature of the environment, the nature of things (hard, soft, bouncy, springy). Much of play is about movement (jumping, skipping, creeping); much of play is about exploring. A great deal of play is about creating, and much of it is about the use of the imagination.

Christine Cooper (Consultant Paediatrician) wrote in (1986)

> 'Whatever their environment, children will absorb some details of people and things around them and will try to make sense of what is happening. But the confused impressions which a chronically neglected child receives are very different from the sense of the world received by a child who is part of a loving, stable family group and who is encouraged to explore, enquire and understand what he or she sees and hears, tastes, smells and feels. The neglected child may have little incentive to explore or to play, has few satisfying relationships, does not receive suitable guidance or controls of behaviour and does not view the world as an interesting place where fun is enjoyed and skills can develop.'

So, these children may also have missed out on play. They, no doubt, will have 'played', but their play did not bring the rich experience it should have done. Cooper (1986) goes on to outline the ways in which various kinds of play help children to develop the full potential of their bodily and mental skills and the enjoyment of themselves relating to the environment. She lists and expands on ten kinds of 'play':

Movement
Exploration and discovery (including physical manipulation)
Initiative play

Constructive play
Pretend or make-believe
Artistic play
Pencil play and practising writing and number-work
Games with rules
Storytelling, reading and enjoyment of picture books
Recreation and hobbies

We cannot give space in this book to replacement therapies concerning the lost experiential 'riches'. However, the importance of the sensory experiences may be recognised if we look at the healing qualities certain therapists have found in sensory and creative materials and experiences.

In 'Windows To Our Children' (1978) Violet Oaklander provides her readers with a wealth of examples in the provision and use of materials and activities which help children to become healed by their involvement with them. Here are a few extracts:

'On **Touch,**

Clay, finger paint, and, water and foot painting provides good tactile experience ---- For touch experimentation, I have gathered a variety of surfaces: sandpaper, velvet, fur, ribbons, rubber, paper, wood, rock, shells, metal, etc. We touch and talk about how each thing feels, what it reminds us of in our lives. Sometimes I place the objects in a bag and ask a child to reach in and pull out something soft or smooth. Then I take my turn with the child telling me what to take out -----.

We have taken off shoes and tried a variety of textures with our feet. We have taken a walk barefoot — indoors and out and talked about how our feet can feel. We've compared the feeling of our feet on cardboard, newspaper, fur, rugs, pillows, sand, grass, leaves, a towel, wood, ----- rice, water. Two children can touch each other's face and report how it felt to do the touching, and how it felt to be touched.

On **Sound**

Here are some exercises to increase children's awareness of the sounds around them.

Sit quietly with eyes closed and allow the sounds you hear to come to you. Notice your feelings as you take in each sound.

Later we can share our impressions. This kind of exercise takes on completely new dimensions in various locations — indoors, in the city, at the beach, in the country.

Talk about sounds. Share which sounds feel harsh, soft, smooth, grating, pleasant, loud, gentle. **What is your favourite thing to hear?** Gibson (1966) is a good book to read to children as a prelude to this exercise.

Match sounds. I have taken some small jars and old medicine bottles and put a variety of objects — rice, beans, thumb tacks, buttons, washers, coins, anything that will fit — in pairs of bottles. I wrap the jars with masking tape or cover them in some way, so that the objects are hidden from sight. The child shakes each bottle and finds its match through the sound it makes.'

And so she goes on. I have taken just a few sentences from each of these 'senses' sections. She has similar helpful ideas concerning taste, smell and sight. Referring to music, on which she has a lot to say, she writes:

'Children enjoy using coloured chiffon scarves as they move to music, and they love to dance around to rock, boogie, and other contemporary rhythms.

Drums are very appealing to children — even those of us who have little skill can create an acceptable beat. You might say, 'show me what kind of drum beat you would make if you felt sad, or happy', or 'Give us a drum beat and see if we can tell what feeling you're having'.'

Maureen Thom (1984) writing about helping children to get back 'In touch with themselves' writes:

'Less threatening, and as a result often more effective, can be the use of materials which stimulate a child's awareness of his or her interaction with the environment: for example, using water, clay, smell, touch. This is a necessary part of developing a **sense of self.** It is also essential to teach children to be aware of the functioning of their own bodies.'

Finally, a quote from Margaret Lowenfeld (1964), a child psychotherapist:

'Small children are in a peculiar position in regard to their own

> bodies. Sensations from them arise almost continually, powerful urges to movement, violent phenomena like vomiting or diarrhoea, noises of their own crying, the feel of substances and the mystery of sleep ----- time also in the sense of process of time has no meaning for them; each experience as it arises, dominates the field of consciousness.'

The reader is referred to several books in our further reading list which will be helpful in learning about ways in which deprived children may be helped to overcome the effects of deprivation, privation and abuse. Incidentally, some writers are distinguishing **privation** (i.e. where a child has **never** had had an opportunity to form affectional bonds) from **deprivation** (where children have experienced some early bonds of affection but where these have for some reason been broken off) see for example Aldgate et al (1988).

More on attachment

Having looked briefly at some of the qualities to be found in good-enough parenting, and having thought about some of the 'lost riches' I would like now to take the concept of **attachment** and consider some aspects of this process and look at how children who have missed-out may also have parts of the 'Self' which appear to be **stuck.**

A lovely simple definition of **attachment** is that provided by Kennell (1976) and quoted in Fahlberg (1981):

> 'Attachment has been defined as 'an affectionate bond between two individuals that endures through space and time and serves to join them emotionally'.

For those readers who have not already studied the subject, let me say that what is referred to in that brief definition above is in fact a very vast, and to some specialists a controversial area of the study of human psychology. This process of **attachment** is not just the sentimental idea we have in mind when we talk about being 'very attached' to some favourite picture or piece of music or our latest automobile.

Attachment by the child to other human beings, usually natural parents, parent substitutes and siblings, has usually taken place by the time the child is about nine months old, and is vitally important in the development of the child, affecting as it does all the developmental modes I have referred to, affective, cognitive, social and motor (in everyday language; emotional, knowing, relating to others, and body control).

Once a child has really become attached in a healthy way (and even to some extent where there are flaws in the attachment- bonding relationship) it is a serious, and sometimes a painful, traumatic and harmful event if separation occurs, as of course it may do in death, or desertion, or intervention by state or local authority powers.

The psychiatrist, John Bowlby (1986) has made a major contribution to our understanding of attachment in children. He writes:

> 'What for convenience I am terming attachment theory is a way of conceptualising the propensity of human beings to make strong affectional bonds to particular others and of explaining the many forms of emotional distress and personality disturbance, including anxiety, anger, depression, and emotional detachment to which unwilling separation and loss give rise.'

He goes on to say:

> 'Advocates of attachment theory argue that many forms of psychiatric disturbance can be attributed either to deviations in the development of attachment behaviour or, more rarely, to failure of its development; and also that the theory casts light on both the origin and treatment of these conditions.'

We must bear these statements in mind when we review the children I have introduced and others who have missed-out in a similar way. Think of the many moves some of these children have had. Think of the quality of the bonding process so far as some parents are concerned. This may help us to understand, when we consider the pain and trauma these children may have experienced, why they may develop conscious or unconscious caution about 'getting close' to people emotionally — if they do 'it may all happen again'.

Attachment and the arousal-relaxation cycles

It often helps to understand complicated processes if we use diagrams to illustrate the way things are said to work.

Naturally, such diagrams greatly simplify the description and they can seldom show us the extent to which other processes impinge on the one we are studying. Nevertheless they are helpful, and I am grateful to Vera Fahlberg and others for originating what we are now calling the **Arousal-relaxation cycles.** These cycles help us to understand the process of attachment which involves, amongst other characteristics, the development in the child of a sense of trust leading to a sense of **security,** and ultimately to attachment.

Although the process I am about to illustrate goes on throughout the first two or three years of childhood, it will be easier if I start right at the beginning with a newborn infant in mind, because (a) the first year is very important, and (b) with a young baby the various physical needs keep coming round in rapid time cycles, as anyone will know who has cared for young babies.

Erikson (1965) has provided us with a chart of what he called crucial development tasks (Fig.1) which a human being needs to achieve from birth to adulthood. You will note that during the first phase, sometime between birth and thirteen months of age a **sense of trust** may be acquired (or achieved). On the other hand, during this first crucial phase — the foundation phase - a basic sense or **feeling** of mistrust (anxiety, apprehension, insecurity etc.) may develop.

How does this basic trust develop?

It is possible to think of different **needs** arising and being met over and over again in the course of a day with a young infant. The baby (and later the older child) will be in different states as these needs arise and are met. We could string these states in a long line, like this:

A. child relaxed → B. child develops a need (hunger) → C. child highly aroused → D. need met e.g. food provided → A. child again relaxed → B. develops a need (uncomfortable or wind) → etc. etc.

This could go on and on!

FIG 1

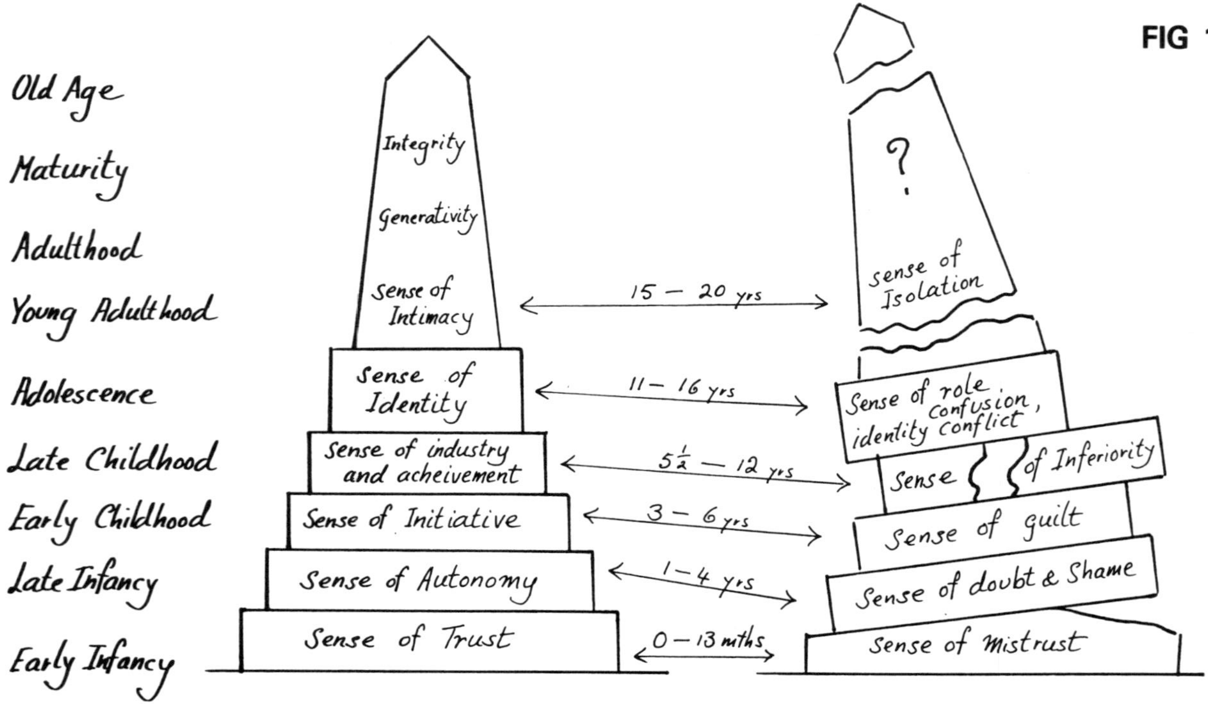

Diagram based on Erikson's crucial development tasks

Instead of stringing these states out in a long line, Fahlberg (1981) put them in a cyclical form (Fig. 2a). So now if you look at my diagram you will see the word **need** at the top of cycle (B). The reader may imagine various needs which will appear there. The need could be for food, or relief from discomfort such as soreness, or wind, etc. At point (C) the child is really in a fully aroused state. She may be crying. Then at point (D) the need is being met. Maybe the child is still not back to being fully relaxed (or as Fahlberg's original diagram had it, **quiescent**) but then we come round to point (A) and the child is relaxed, or quiescent. No doubt this sounds like a 'perfect' baby ('ours was not as easy as that!') Nevertheless, the diagram makes the point that although comfort and discomfort may come and go frequently even during the course of one day, the discomfort or pain will not (in good-enough parenting) get worse and worse and never be relieved. Provided we are dealing with a healthy child the **usual** course of events is as illustrated in the arousal- relaxation cycle. Remember that the child helps this cycle to go round. The child, if all is well, will cry. If completely ignored he will scream in frustration. He will demand his rights!

I am deliberately leaving out the complications, of course, although it is easy to see that a child could learn to push the cycle round to the extent of over controlling the parents. But in wise, good-enough parenting the general feeling, or 'sense of' produced in the long run is a feeling of security and trust. The child has no words for this experience, but in Erikson's language a **sense of trust** is achieved. However, many of the children this book is about did not have their needs met, and they finished their first year of life with a **sense of mistrust.**

Attachment can take place if this cycle of needs, and of changing states, is functioning to a satisfactory degree, but the reader must remember that the child's needs include all those hard to define but extremely important emotional and social needs such as talking to, bouncing, looking at, smiling at, cuddling and, later on, explaining, encouraging, listening to **and** correcting the child whilst upholding her in love.

Now look at the circle which Fahlberg has called **The positive interaction cycle** (Fig 2b). In this case we see that the parent is the main subject for driving the cycle round, and because of what happens the child develops those feelings of **self-worth** and **self-esteem** I have already referred to.

At the top of the **positive interaction cycle** you will see the

FIG 2A

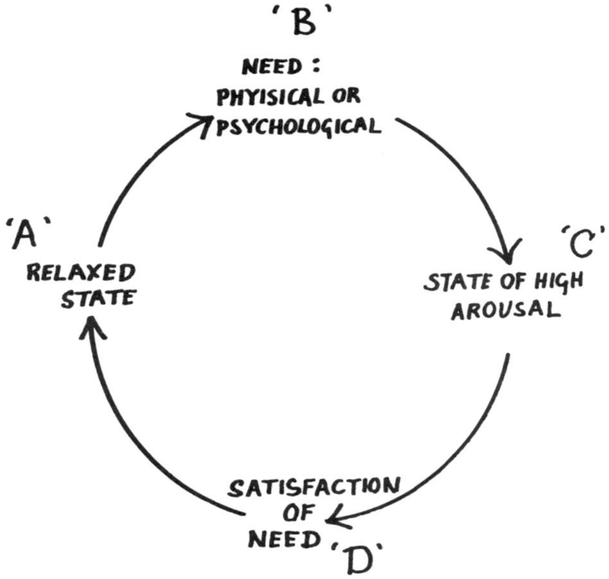

Cycle of interaction leading to Security, Trust and Attachment.

FIG 2B

Cycle of interaction leading to experience of Self-Worth and Self-Esteem in Child

(after Vera Fahlberg)

statement 'Parent initiates positive interactions with child'. In the early infant phase these will include interactions I have just mentioned as **needs** of the child: 'talking-to' (the baby may not know what the parent is **saying** but he will **feel** what she or he is communicating!). Smiling-at, bouncing, cuddling and many other forms of interaction will at first be initiated by the caregivers (and others, including siblings). You know the fuss that is made when the first genuine response smile comes from the baby! But later on the needs will include story-telling, playing games, telling the child that something is safe or not safe. These two cycles give us the basics for bonding (Parents) and attaching (Child). Of this **positive interaction cycle** Fahlberg (1981) writes:

> 'We have seen that the arousal-relaxation cycle is initiated by the child's needs and that successful completion of this cycle contributes to bonding between mother and child. However, the extent to which the mother initiates interactions with the infant also influences the attachment between them. ------ There is some evidence that these sorts of special interactions between mother and child contribute more to the bonds between them than do the kind of interactions that occur around meeting the child's physical needs. For example, Ainsworth (1952) feels that social interactions, not routine care, are the most important part of mothering. The more social interactions an infant has with someone, the more strongly attached he becomes to that person.'

These responses to the child's needs, and these positive interactions by the parents and others also represent **riches** of the non-things type. These riches, some of our children never had.

Attachment and children who are 'stuck'

Children of all ages, and also adults, may react to circumstances (to frustration, or competition for attention and affection, etc.) as if these cycles were not going round. Indeed our concept of the 'stuck' child includes behaviour where the child, on account of the failure in his early life arousal-relaxation experience, may remain with basic inner feelings of anger because his reactions remain 'stuck' at point C (arousal) and he is incapable of pushing that cycle round towards **relaxation** since he also destroys attempts by others to help him. Alternatively a child's response may be to become adaptive (perhaps appearing as a child who never makes demands and is 'so good you wouldn't know you had him') and in effect he remains 'stuck' at point (B) where needs are felt but never expressed.

On account of what I have said concerning emotional retardation (as well as motor and cognitive retardation) I will also refer to children being 'stuck', or part of their development being 'stuck' at a younger age (chronologically speaking) emotionally.

Fahlberg (1984) categorises the way children may become 'stuck' thus:

- Developmental retardation (Physical, cognitive, affective).
- Children who have developed an abnormal (maladaptive) way of behaving (their feelings remain concentrated at one point on the arousal-relaxation cycle)
- Children who have not resolved separation issues or worked through feelings of 'loss'
- Children who are 'stuck' in their ability to conceptualise or move on from infantile forms of thinking.

(My paraphrasing of all categories)

Anxious attachment

For some of these children the statement, 'These riches some of our children never had', used above, may be rather misleading. It could in some cases be rather like saying that a child suffering from malnutrition never had any meals. Of course he probably had 'meals' but the meals were usually deficient in essential elements so perhaps the child failed to get enough vitamin B. Most of the children who show signs of having been rejected, neglected or emotionally deprived will show some indications of acknowledging an attachment figure, even when they are experiencing emotional tension and stress, and even when running away from home.

What we may be faced with in these circumstances is what Bowlby (1986) has called **anxious attachment.** The child has 'attached' to the only constant caregivers known to her, yet the 'attachment' itself may sometimes be riddled with child destroying relationships; with what some specialists would call pathological relationships, and 'pathogenic parenting'.

Bowlby (1986) has written:

'Many of those referred to psychiatrists are anxious, insecure individuals, usually described as over-dependent or immature.

Under stress they are apt to develop neurotic symptoms, depression or phobia. Research shows them to have been exposed to at least one, usually more than one, of certain typical patterns of pathogenic parenting, which include:

- One or both parents being persistently unresponsive to the child's care-eliciting behaviour and/or actively disparaging and rejecting him.
- Discontinuities of parenting, occurring more or less frequently, including periods in hospital or institution.
- Persistent threats by parents not to love the child, used as a means of controlling him.
- Threats by parents to abandon the family, used either as a method of disciplining the child or as a way of coercing a spouse.
- Threats by one parent either to desert or even to kill the other or else to commit suicide (each of them more common than might be supposed).
- Inducing a child to feel guilty by claiming that his behaviour is or will be responsible for the parent's illness or death.

Any of these experiences can lead a child, an adolescent or an adult to live in constant anxiety lest he lose his attachment figure and, as a result, to have a low threshold for manifesting attachment behaviour. The condition is best described as one of **anxious attachment**' (my emphasis).

Children may show signs of satisfactory attachment, or anxious attachment, or in some cases no real attachment to anyone. Does it matter? Why is attachment thought to be so important?

Apart from what has already been stated in relation to poor or anxious attachment, and what I have implied in my descriptions of poorly attached children, there are several important reasons for considering the quality of the attachment (and bonding) process as critical and vital to child and adult development.

Consider, for example, the following list of attainments and how vital they really are. This is a list provided by Fahlberg (1981). I shall comment briefly here on some of the attainments, but the reader is reminded that behaviour and its relationship to attachment is an extensive subject for further study:

Attachment helps the child:—
Attain his full intellectual potential
Sort out what he perceives

Think logically
Develop a conscience
Become self-reliant
Cope with stress and frustration
Handle fear and worry
Develop future relationships
Reduce jealousy

I is easy to read or 'flip' over a list like this without the full impact hitting us. Take for example, the fourth attainment 'develop a conscience'. What is being stated here is that in the case of certain children whose behaviour ('lying' 'stealing' 'cruelty' etc.) leads to so much anguish, adult anger, despair and maybe finally a further experience of 'rejection', the inner control of these children ('conscience') is missing because of this lack of attachment or this **anxious** attachment.

Now that is a very bold statement to make, and if it is true it is a very far reaching statement. Even though I think it contains an important element of truth, I am also sure that we have to be careful of the way we use these ideas. So, although I want the reader to hold on to that message, the importance of attachment in the development of the **conscience,** I also want to say that we are here touching upon a very complex subject, an aspect of personality development that the various schools of psychology have contributed to.

In fact, few of the explanations for the development of **conscience** or 'moral development' have much to say about **feelings** or the affect, although some writers are now emphasising these aspects. Helen Haste (1987) is an example.

I think that there are very many important **bits** belonging to these huge psychological jigsaws, and the bit Vera Fahlberg has picked out here is very important to our study. So, without deviating and turning this into a text book on child psychology, let me provide the reader with a few quotes by way of emphasising the link between the child's 'inner controls' and the parenting he or she experienced.

First, Judy Dunn, the well known psychologist and writer (1984):-

'What this research has shown is that a firm and reasonably consistent response to children's physical aggression or unkindness

> **in the context of a loving and warm relationship between parents and child** seems to work most effectively in encouraging children's altruism and sensitivity to others.' (My emphasis).

In a study of 'good boys' in a delinquency area Scarpitti (1960) learnt something about these boys who had developed an **inner control,** and were able to avoid delinquency. Hurlock (1964) reports on this:

> it was found that those who were 'insulated' from the mores of their social group had developed internalized law-abiding norms because of favourable home training and **the satisfaction they derived from their parents' affection.** Those who were not 'insulated' and whose behaviour was regulated by environmental pressures rather than by internalized standards came mainly from homes where moral training was meagre and where **parent-child relationships were poor.**'

Michael Rutter, a leading practitioner and research worker in the field of child psychiatry writes (1975):

> 'Incorporation of parental standards (with modification) is more likely when there is a good relationship with the child and, probably, when the methods of discipline used convey the message that what the child does really matters to the parent because **he** (the child) matters.'

Some of my readers will be caring for children who 'seem to have no conscience' and who show no indications of guilt or shame. Those children, often desperate to belong despite their seemingly affectionless or aggressive attitudes, have a tremendous task to achieve in terms of how they **feel** towards those who are caring for them, and how they **feel** about their own behaviour. Their parents, or foster or adoptive parents also have so much to accomplish. It is not easy, but the changes **can** take place — in time.

Well, that was just one of Vera Fahlberg's attainments associated with attachment. Read the others over again and consider their importance. What about the third one down, 'think logically'? and the sixth one 'cope with stress and frustration'? If your child has had attachment problems she may well be affected negatively in these areas of development. Even if she is helped at home by your understanding and patience, think of the stress and frustration at school. Think of Vivien I described in chapter one, and her 'bad' behaviour at school, and the frustration she could not cope with, and Vivien's school report: 'Could be good at drama, and likes it, but deliberately disrupts the class and so is excluded from this year's production'.

In this chapter I have looked at some of the missed-out bits in the lives of children who have been deprived of a good-enough parenting experience. Some children who have suffered deprivation, or strictly speaking **privation,** are now being cared for and receiving the nurture and guidance they should have had from infancy, but because of the psychological damage done earlier they still experience, and present 'problems'.

In chapter three I want to look at the sort of experiences our children have had and which they should not have had. Not the **lost riches** but the **damaging lumber.**

CHAPTER THREE

Damaging Lumber

When it comes to **damaging lumber** it is easy for us to be attracted by the headline stuff, the physically abused and the sexually abused children, and all the drama of court appearances and media concentration, not to mention media twists and biases. I shall be looking at this sort of lumber in this chapter. However, there are other damaging experiences which are easily overlooked and which the general public probably never become aware of, and even many caregivers may overlook.

We shall, for example, consider the sort of damaging experiences a child may undergo when, oddly enough, she is taken into **care.** I am referring here to factors which are inherent in poor quality 'social care'. Unfortunately there is a lot of poor quality social care about. One kind of damaging lumber in the poor quality care experience is the number of moves from one unsuitable **placement** to another unsuitable placement, or from a suitable to an unsuitable **placement.**

There are even more subtle forms of damaging lumber. These may be dressed up to look like good quality nurturing experiences. Some children, for example, have experienced a special overpowering, personality-crushing form of 'love' and 'bonding' from a parent figure. This is damaging lumber just as much as physical or sexual abuse.

Physical abuse

Children seldom experience physical abuse, or cruelty as it is sometimes called, on its own. It nearly always goes along with other experiences such as violence in the family between the adults, emotional rejection, poverty, sexual abuse, alcoholism, mental illness or mental handicap in the adults, or in one of the parents. In describing physical abuse in this section, however, I shall do as I had to do in chapter two when considering personality. I shall give an abstract and describe, in the main, just the physical violence and the sort of injuries sustained by children.

There are various **typical** or characteristic injuries or scars and bruisings connected with physical abuse of children. We need not differentiate these nor elaborate on them here but they include bite-marks (i.e. made by the teeth and leaving crescent shaped series of marks) cigarette burns, strap-marks or buckle marks, and various bruise formations. There are also **typical** internal injuries ranging from bone fracture to head and brain injury (eg. subdural haematoma, where internal bleeding may result from giving a child a violent shake or a blow on the head).

John, whom I introduced in chapter one, was a child who experienced particularly harsh punishment: 'Not just the odd tap on the hand but brutal punishment. Punishment for John seemed to have been a built-in characteristic of the universe. It wasn't only that physical punishment was practised upon him by so called 'sadistic' people, though that was damaging enough ------' etc.

Tony who came into care with his sister, Judy, was another child who had experienced physical abuse; 'When he came into care there were lots of bruises all over Tony's body. There were weals round his wrists and ankles where he had been bound, screaming, to the bed or other pieces of furniture'. Then there was young Paul, the over-active little boy: 'Talking about being tied to things. Paul had experienced this literally when he lived with Marlene — she dealt with his over-activity by tying him to his bed.' etc.

The Royal Society For the Prevention of Cruelty to Children came into existence in order to protect children from just this sort of **damaging lumber.** Here is a quotation from one of their publications (Allen and Morton 1963):

> 'Three little girls had the misfortune to be born to the wrong type of army parent. To a small though significant proportion of men the services give an identity without which they are lost and if they have risen in rank and learned the glory of a little power, civilian life and in particular family life alarms them. They meet the threat to their picture of themselves as powerful and always-to-be-obeyed people by imposing a false and totally im-

possible set of standards on their children ---- the only people too small and too weak to retaliate ----- the words 'sergeant-major type of parent' immediately bring to mind a family whose children know only discipline without love, arbitrary decisions without explanation or reason, and no praise for achievement at all.

In the case of these three sisters the situation was exacerbated by the fact that their mother, unlike most wives in this position whose immediate instinct is to compensate by over-indulgence behind their husband's back, was sufficiently hard to be able to sit on the sofa and laugh as her husband beat the two elder girls with an army belt while they screamed and begged him to stop.

When the case finally came to light, marks of the brass buckle could be seen all over their bodies in various degrees of freshness and fading. They were ten and eleven years old.'

Sadly, there are many thousands of children whose physical suffering goes on without the NSPCC or the public, or even the neighbours realising it. Most of these children do not experience the extreme cruelty leading to death and the subsequent arrest of the perpetrators or to the arrest of parents on charges of cruelty or grievous bodily harm. Most suffer enough to be psychologically damaged or to eventually run away from home but not enough to stand out as needing help. Some, those like the ones I've introduced to the reader in chapter one for example, do suffer more and are put into **care** by the Courts. They need the help of loving caregivers or the help of people who can really rehabilitate them **and** help their offending parents. They have been damaged by this kind of lumber (together with other 'lumber' and the loss of so many 'riches').

To help the reader appreciate some of the risks to which children are exposed so far as physical abuse is concerned, it will be salutary to read a few extracts from some of the Reports made concerning children who did not manage to survive their treatment. These children were either 'in the care of the local authority' at the time of their deaths or they were well known to the health and welfare departments and had been in and out of care and were known to be 'at risk' at the time of their deaths.

The name of Maria Colwell has come down to us from 1973. This little girl was nearly eight years old when on the night of 6/7

January of that year she succumbed at the hands of her step-father. She probably succumbed fairly easily because by that date she had experienced months of severe physical abuse. She had been severely physically punished; and she had been made to undertake work beyond her (failing) physical strength, and she had not been adequately fed. The Report (Colwell 1974) states:

> 'On 27th Miss Tester, whose evidence we have referred to before, spent the evening baby sitting for the Kepples (the parents) and went up to see Maria in bed. From her evidence about that occasion, we gained the impression of a withdrawn, quiet, sad little girl who might metaphorically be said to have turned her face to the wall.'

Elsewhere:

> 'On 2nd January 1973 Mrs. Kepple returned home to find Maria with a black eye and Mr. Kepple told her she had fallen downstairs. On 6th January Mr. Kepple came in at 11.30 p.m. and the events which formed the basis of the indictment against him occurred:'

Then later:

> 'The following morning the Kepples took Maria in a pram to the hospital where she was found to be dead. The post mortem showed that she was severely bruised all over the body and head and had sustained internal injuries to the stomach. There was a healing fracture of one rib. The bruising which was described by Professor Cameron as the worst he had ever seen, was of variable age up to 10 to 14 days at the most, but the majority dated from within 48 hours. The stomach was empty and the body weighed 36 lbs (she should have weighed between 46 and 50 lbs). She had in fact grown one inch and lost over 5 lbs since her last medical examination on 14th August 1971, seventeen months before her death.'

Some children suffer a combination of **neglect** and cruelty. They miss out on the nurturing riches I have spoken of in chapter two, and they experience a lot of unwanted lumber in the form of events they should not experience. Lucie Gates (1982 Gates) was one such child: on pages 32/33 of the report we read:-

> 'It was agreed that the Inspector should make further inquiries and visit the Gates family to assess the situation. She obtained written statements from five neighbours. Their main complaints were:
>
> - Linda's flat was filthy (Linda is Lucie's mother)
> - Her children were dirty and neither properly clothed nor fed.
> - She had an assortment of male visitors.
> - Sometimes she left the children alone until the early hours of the morning while she visited a public house.
> - She hit the children excessively and without cause.'

The reader should always bear in mind that the parents themselves may have very real problems, social and psychological, which impede the development of parenting roles and even parental feelings. The report on Lucie Gates (page 49) states:

> 'Nursing staff at the hospital reported to Social Worker 2 that Linda Gates did not appear to know the basics of motherhood, particularly how to feed the baby despite having had three other children............Social Worker 2, in her May 1977 summary report, wrote: "Linda did not take to Lucie. She was a small, fragile looking baby that Linda was frightened of."

On page 87 of the report we read:

> 'Neighbour Two described an incident in Hook Lane School playground, said to have happened in March 1979, when Linda hit Lucie round the head with a clenched fist. This neighbour said that later she had noticed bruising on Lucie's head'.

In the end it was a combination of neglect (children left on their own) and an accident, an electric fire falling on the little girl, then aged two years and eight months, which brought about her death. From pages 93-95:

> 'At about 11.40 p.m. Neighbour One heard Mary (sister) screaming in the court outside. She went with Mary to the Gate's flat.

Smoke was coming from the living room. The neighbour found Lucie beneath an electric fire and dragged her clear ------ an ambulance left John Newton Court with Lucie at 12.16 a.m.'

The report then describes the extent of Lucie's terrible burns and then states:-

'She died in hospital on the 19th June 1979.'

This makes rather sickening reading and there is no need to subject my readers to more of the same, although there continues to be a fair amount of the same, including Tyra Henry who died in September 1984, and Kimberley Carlile who died in June 1986. But these are children who actually died. Many more children suffer neglect and/or physical abuse but survive, although quite a lot of them find their way into public care and become the sort of children already described in chapter one.

Readers, especially those who are caring for deprived and disturbed children, will be concerned to know what effects physical abuse, including harsh punishment, has on the personality development of the children. This of course is a very broad subject and the reader is referred to our **further reading** list. However, depending upon many variables, including the child's basic temperament and the sort of abuse (continual, sporadic, 'sadistic', disciplinary etc.) we may expect to find a wide range of behavioural abnormalities extending from the passive, watchful, shy child who hardly ever smiles, through to the hyperactive, over anxious, aggressive and hostile child or young person. Between these extremes we may find the abused child who is over adaptive, that is to say he attempts to comply with everyone's wishes or what he sees as their wishes. He is prepared to accept whatever happens, and to be passive and 'obedient'. He seems not to feel pain or excessive cold or discomfort to the same degree as other children.

The Kempes when writing about physically abused children (1978) head one of the sections 'DEMON' SYMPTOMS, and go on to say:

'Not all children who have been abused are compliant and anxious to please. At least one fourth of the young children (and more, we suspect, of the older ones) are negative, aggressive, and often hyperactive as well. These children seem veritable demons, who have responded to the experience of aggression with almost manic activity ----------- The only attention they seem

> to try for is negative, and their language is even more aggressive than their behaviour.'

Some young children may even present with symptoms described in the syndrome of 'frozen watchfulness', the very opposite of over- aggression. The Kempes, referring to Christopher Ounsted's 'frozen watchfulness' syndrome say:

> 'These children stare continually revealing (later when they feel more free to talk) a remarkable memory for physical surroundings and events. It is as if they can take nothing for granted, but must always be on the watch to avoid trouble or to try to please. Their eyes continually scan the environment for danger, while at the same time their faces are immobile; there are no spontaneous smiles and almost no eye contact.'

However, many people caring for children (and adults) who have experienced violence, including harsh 'punishment' in their earlier childhood, are faced not with 'frozen watchfulness' (although that may have been present when the child came into care as an infant) but with hostility and aggression beyond what is often found during adolescence, and beyond the usual influences of a violent sub-culture, and some of these older children seem to carry a sort of **smouldering anger,** a bitter resentfulness which often surfaces (in school, in a group situation and in the family) and even at the best of times is only just below the surface.

There is evidence that many perpetrators of violence have had violence inflicted upon them. They are both the perpetrators and the victims. It seems also that **care** or **kindness** or **love** (choose your word) 'hurts' certain young people. They can't take it! Emotionally it 'burns' them.

Anthony Storr (1985) makes the following observations concerning violence generating violence:-

> 'The fourth factor which influences people in the direction of cruelty is the treatment which they themselves experienced when children ------------ It seems probable that those who have been harshly treated as children are particularly prone to treat other human beings with cruelty, both because they have a particular need to establish dominance and because they wish to be revenged.'

Other practitioners and researchers have directed attention to the **frequency** and **continuity** of harsh punishment and to **inconsistency** in disciplinary measures as contributing to anti-social and hostile behaviour, (eg. one parent being lax while the other is tough, or parents permitting behaviour one day while lashing out physically the next day for the same behaviour). Rutter (1975) Glueck, S and E (1952) Meadows, S. (1986).

Remember, we are not talking here of an occasional slap or being sent out of the room, etc., we are talking of the effects of cruel, brutish treatment with, as likely as not, confusing inconsistency. We must also remember that these experiences of cruelty and violence (damaging lumber) do not come separately as a rule but are experienced in a world devoid of a consistent display of affection or love, Shirley (1963).

As I said at the beginning of this section, physical abuse may lead to personality traits other than hostile aggression. Depressive disorders, which in turn may be associated with alcoholism, are also associated with overharsh discipline, cruelty etc. Furthermore, depression may follow harsh discipline even where there is no history of profound misbehaviour in childhood, Holmes and Robins (1987) Pfeffer, Newcorn et, al (1989).

Before considering another form of **damaging lumber** it may be helpful for readers to know that there is a growing bank of literature to indicate that 'recovery' and development towards 'normality' may be expected even in the most extreme cases of prolonged neglect and physical cruelty **provided** an environment offering nurtural care, empathy, patience and knowledge is found for the child. Some emotional as well as physical scars may remain, and of course much depends upon the strengths of the placement.

Sexual abuse

Here are some words written by a woman who was sexually abused by her father when she was a little girl of seven, and consistently thereafter into later teen-age:

> 'I wanted to murder my body so that I might somehow, be able to continue in the world with only a brain — it was my body's fault that this was happening to me.'

Those words were written by Charlotte Vale Allen (1983) to describe her feelings during moments of sexual assault by her father. She explains, also, that she used to be able to go into a kind of trance state, a vacuum 'where my physical self failed to exist and my mind rested like a bird on the high wires'.

Here is a child certainly having experiences she should never have had, and we can see the way she is attempting to maintain the balance of her mind by a splitting off process. In this chapter, as already explained, I am emphasising the **damaging lumber** — things that should not have been experienced. But in many cases, including Charlotte's, these go along with a childhood devoid of those **riches** we spoke of in chapter two. So earlier in her book we find her describing her need for a consistent show of love from her mother, and her anguish at the violence of the rows between her parents. There were times when her mother was in a 'good mood, calm and prepared to play a game,' then:

> 'I'd feel a welling, almost a sad happiness. Maybe she did love me after all and it was me — the things I sometimes said and did — it was my fault she didn't love me all the time.'

Notice the feeling of **guilt** produced in the child. These 'non- guilty' guilt feelings can later contribute to depressive feelings (springing from the unconscious) which may stay around for a long time, even into adulthood.

I have used the extracts, above, from Charlotte Vale Allen's book because I want the reader to appreciate that in many cases of child sexual abuse, most I would say, we are faced not only with some nasty physical-sexual event, but with a complex network of events which may involve psychological factors in the child (and the later adult) such as guilt, feeling 'dirty', anger, fear etc., but will also include what I call psycho-social factors. For instance, I have known family situations where the father of an abused child was sent to prison, and the child was put into a children's centre (residential), both events producing guilt and anxiety, and then, when the child was returned home, most of her near relatives 'cut her off' and blamed her for her father's imprisonment. So we are not dealing with isolated incidents (however traumatic some of these may be) which give the child a bad experience, but where, apart from that experience, she will enjoy support and normality in family life. We are often dealing with malfunctioning families as well.

Furthermore, whatever others may feel about the abuser, it is often, for the child, not simply a matter of rejecting him, for quite often, going along with the trauma and the feelings resulting from it, there is an actual desire to be loved — to experience normal parental protection and affection from the abuser. This introduces feelings of **betrayal,** not that the child can put her feelings into such words. Another complication is that too sudden and too strong a signal of outrage and repulsion from a well meaning adult, may actually complicate the child's already confused state of love-hate. Charlotte Vale Allen goes on to say that when her father was abusing her, including making her have oral sex:

> 'I wanted him dead. Or I wanted him to turn into a father and love me ------ I'd house a big bubble of anger that seemed to fill my chest completely; I visualised acts of revenge and bitterly relished images of myself brandishing a knife from the kitchen to stab him to death.'

She explains, elsewhere, the love-hate feelings she carried. At times, when her dad was treating her in a proper way, she felt a bit like a protected, non-abused child. She often thought about the love experience of being a little girl enjoying a 'real dad' playing real games with her and taking her out proudly, and she compared these thoughts to her feelings of hate for the dad whom she at those other times felt as nasty, abusing and unnatural.

Many of the children and young people in care, and whom our readers are likely to meet if they are childcare workers or foster parents, are most likely to have experienced poor infant nurture, family disruption and emotional rejection as well as sexual abuse. It would be difficult in most cases to tease out the strands of their lives and to ascribe **that** bit of behaviour to sexual abuse and **this** bit of behaviour to the poor quality of their attachment-bonding experiences. Here are some further extracts, this time from the account given by another woman, Norma Symonds (1987) who was sexually abused as a child by outsiders. In this case I shall, so to speak, tell her story back to front by giving readers the later extracts first and working back to the early part of her life as a little girl. Here she speaks as a young woman in London:

> 'If I lacked a bed for the night I travelled round and round the Circle Line till it closed in the small hours, then moved on to the all-night chemist at 'The Dilly' to get my stuff, retiring to the women's lavatory by Trafalgar Square to inject myself.

I was 'registered' unofficially with a doctor in the Stockwell area who prescribed for a few addicts. He doled out the drugs - not always heroin. I could manage quite well with Valium, Mogadon or other sleepers. He kept me damped down and quiescent, but as he signed prescriptions gave mild lectures — "This is going to kill you someday. You need help" — "I couldn't care less" I mumbled ---------- Hallucinating badly, afraid to sleep at night in case I died, I pushed myself along till I collapsed in some back alley, or joined the human wrecks who littered the steps around Eros.'

A little before this she had seduced a well-meaning, respectable married woman who had taken her into her own home:

'Mrs. Smith came in and prayed for me. Then she sat by my bed to give me a cuddle and reassure me. She was trying to help, but some influence from the pit in me took control. "Hold me" I instructed her, and she slipped into bed with me. She didn't realise what was happening between us but I did, and I started to make overtures to her which, to her own surprise, she began slowly to respond to.

"You're going to hate yourself for this tomorrow, Mrs. S." I thought, but I wanted what she could give me — **a maternal** love. I didn't know of any other way of getting it from her.' (my emphasis).

The reader will notice Norma felt the need for a **maternal love.** Continuing backwards with some further extracts:

"You're back, I see." My mother stood unsmiling at my bedside. My father wouldn't come. It was evident that they had virtually rejected me. They couldn't see the lost little girl inside who still craved reassurance that somebody loved her.'

By eight years of age Norma had a need for cigarettes, and for money to purchase them. She'd earlier gravitated to a gang of boys:

'We smoked our cigarettes behind the bike shed. I was copying my parents who both smoked, and, since I wasn't given much pocket money (I was also) getting threepences for Woodbines out of the boys by satisfying their curiosity in the matter of certain physical differences between the sexes.'

Later when she wanted more money and she was now about eleven — I'm skipping backwards and forwards at this bit — she was used by an oldish man, a widower:

> 'Then he sat me on his knee and began a touching game familiar to me from my assignations at the bike sheds. Only this was an adult version. I was frozen with fear and shame.'

Later with a young man:

> 'It didn't alarm me. Stupidly I began to flirt, leading him on, as I had learned to do with Mr. C. It just seemed like a game grown men liked to play ----- Suddenly, he grabbed me and pushed me down on the ground. He had his hand over my mouth so that I couldn't scream. I tried to struggle, but to no avail. I can remember the tearing pain as he raped me.'

Back still further in her life:

> 'I went to Sunday School, and Church, and was a Brownie, I had a good home; the scene was set for a happy life, yet something was wrong. Looking back now I realise that what I craved was love and affection, and I didn't seem to have it from anyone ------There was no creeping into bed with my mother, when I wanted a bit of company in the night. When I fell and grazed my knee ---- there was no comforting lap for me to be nursed on till the tears dried.'

And now we are nearly back to the beginning. Sometimes children are wrongly placed. Sometimes people are accepted as adopters or foster parents who may themselves be 'damaged' emotionally and, as we have seen in chapter one, are unable to give the full nurturing a child needs. In Norma's case, after a piece of misbehaviour the bomb is dropped:

> 'She (mother) was waiting for me to say something, but I couldn't think of anything to say. I wasn't sorry for my misdeeds; only sorry she had heard about them. I suppose that riled her, and made her speak as she did, tossing a bomb into my life in the most casual way possible, without heat, or anger but with deadly aim.

> "Oh well," she said, "I suppose it's to be expected. You're not ours anyway. You're adopted."

This was when Norma was about seven or eight years old.

She describes her feelings:

> 'That piece of information, kept from me till then, exploded, shattering my life. One minute I was a daughter in disgrace ------ the next instant I was nobody, belonging nowhere. I felt numb, dead. We completed our walk in silence.'

Later her mother 'softened a bit' and tried to do a bit of repair:

> "I don't know anything about your real mother" she told me. "But you weren't a pretty baby then. You were bruised and sickly and we had to take you over to the other side of Glasgow for heat treatment."

So we now have a picture of a damaged baby, of an infant who missed out on those **riches** so vital to the early months of life. Because of this, and maybe her adoptive parents' own personalities, there may well have been attachment and bonding problems after Norma was placed for adoption. Probably her adopters tried their best but did not have the help and advice which should have been available. Just one last quote concerning Norma's feelings after this event:

> '----- my life was all wrong. It was turning inward on itself, as all the natural outlets were being sealed off. If nobody liked me, or loved me, if I couldn't achieve anything, and didn't belong anywhere, then what did anything matter? I began to gravitate to the boys. They accepted me ---------.'

The scope of child sexual abuse

This part of our subject could be quite extensive, and the reader who wishes to go into it more deeply is advised to consult the literature, including the material listed in our **further reading** section.

Those who are caring for children; those who are placing children and selecting caregivers, and those who have a protective role need to know:

- Who are the perpetrators of child sexual abuse?
- Where does sexual abuse take place?
- What forms does it take — what do we mean by sexual abuse?

The answers to these questions will vary, of course, depending on how one defines the term 'sexual abuse'. But there are lots of other problems connected with research into this subject. Many pieces of research are based, for example, on collecting information from adults about their childhood experiences, and there is evidence that many people interviewed do not reveal their sexual abuse experiences (La Fontaine J, 1989). Then, again, in some countries 'sexual abuse' is a notifiable offence whereas in Great Britain, for example, even if researchers write to doctors and psychiatrists and other workers, the response will often be low on account of the policy of protecting confidentiality.

The percentage figures (of children sexually abused) in populations vary, therefore, between 0.3 and 38, which is fairly meaningless as it stands.

However, one reliable American study puts the United States figure at between 10-14 per cent which would indicate that between 60,000 to 100,000 children are sexually abused each year in the U.S.A. (Bander, Fein and Bishop 1982).

For our purpose, bearing in mind the care of disturbed children, and the need which may exist for clarification of feelings and relearning of social behaviour, it is well to use a broad definition. Adams and Fay (1981) have given us the following definition:

> 'Sexual assault means the forcing of sexual contact. This can involve handling the child's genitals or requests for sexual handling by an older child or adult. Sometimes the contact is oral sex. Sexual contact includes attempts at penetration of the vagina or anus. Sometimes actual penetration by penis, but also fingers and objects can be used. Some assaults involve no physical contact. A child may be forced to look at the genitals of an older child or adult; forced to watch adults having sex; forced to perform sexual acts in front of an adult(s); forced to undress or otherwise expose themselves.'

Gerrylin Smith (1989) after quoting this definition say:

> 'I would add "spied on and photographed in private personal situations." It is important to know this detail because you must be prepared for what a child or young person might reveal to you.'

The reader will understand that this definition goes a long way beyond a legal definition of sexual abuse, but to stick to a legal definition would be to overlook much of the sexual exploitations of children. There are even cases in which the child or young person was forced to have a sexual involvement with an animal.

Children are mostly abused sexually within their own families and most often by family members. The greatest number of children who are sexually abused are abused by their father (about 31 per cent) other relatives account for about another 30 per cent. These 'relatives' include grandfathers, uncles, cousins, stepfathers and male cohabitees. This may give a very different picture to the one the reader previously had in mind. Also, psychologically speaking, it introduces further **damaging lumber** on account of the feelings of betrayal or confusion arising in the child, not that we want to play down the attacks, some of them isolated incidents, which occur due to strangers and acquaintances from outside the family. These, incidentally would appear in some research projects to account for about 20 per cent of cases (Community Care 1988). Jill Waterman and Rob Lusk (1986) have said:

> 'There is general agreement that children are sexually abused by people close to them — relatives, step-relatives, friends of the family, neighbours, and authority figures. The perverted stranger in a trench-coat offering candy to children is clearly not the culprit in the sexual abuse of most young children. It has been found that 75-80 per cent of sexual abuse occurs within 'affinity systems' — families, relatives, friends, and neighbours.'

'I wanted to murder my body'

What does sexual abuse do to children? Moreover, what does this form of childhood damaging lumber do to the adult who eventually emerges from the child? From what has been quoted in these pages recording the experiences and **feelings** of Charlotte Vale

Allen and Norma Symonds our readers will already have some idea of the sort of damage that can result.

I almost headed this subsection **The Effects of Sexual Abuse,** and that would have been appropriate because that is what we shall be briefly looking at here, but it sounded academic and possibly statistical, and it would have failed to emphasise the most important outcome of the damage — the **feelings** the person (child, adult) is left with, and feelings are **real,** so that is why I fell back on Charlotte Vale Allen's words, 'I wanted to murder my own body'.

Then there is the confusion about how to interact person to person. When a child is wrongly **programmed** (a harsh mechanical word but used advisedly) by trusted adults they are likely not only to experience betrayal but to have to **unlearn** that programme of social and physical interaction and **relearn** how to interact. We saw this in chapter one with Judy and her brother, Tony:

> 'Judy is still somewhat confused, but not as confused as she was at home or with the Burrows. At first with Bob and Alice it was even worse than when she first went to the Burrows. Then, at least, she **thought** she knew what to do, but this time she cannot use even the ploys she had learnt at home, so what **do** people do to get loved and wanted, and to belong?'

However, all these experiences are very personal, very individual, very special, unhappily unique and belonging to that particular child or adult, so it would be difficult to estimate the damage done to individual children, or to list sexual offence in order of damage effect. Often, also, the behaviour observed in children who have been sexually abused, the emotional states described by them or attributed to them by experts, are the same as those resulting allegedly from the other forms of **damaging lumber** and **lost riches** we have also looked at.

Rob Lusk and Jill Waterman, et al (1986) writing about the effects of sexual abuse on pre-school children state that 'There is an extraordinary amount of variability in the effects described in the literature' and they say that, from the various studies, it appears that **guilt** (or shame) is a common reaction:

> 'Children tend to blame themselves for the abuse (and) may feel especially guilty if they enjoyed aspects of it.'

Anxiety also occurs a lot in the findings of these studies, and, especially with pre-school children, **fear** goes along very frequently with anxiety. Such fear can be later turned into various phobias.

Another emotional (i.e. affective) reaction found by many researches is **anger,** which is commonly directed towards both parents. This anger may be carried over against the parents when the abused person has become an adult.

There are also many psychosomatic problems reported. By **psychosomatic** we mean various physical illnesses and conditions, and malfunctionings which appear to have psychological 'causes'. These include stomachaches, headaches, wetting and soiling pants or bed, hypochondriasis, tics, and hysterical seizures.

The reader will have noticed that many of the 'effects' outlined here in connection with sexual abuse were also listed as effects in connection with physical abuse. Furthermore, from the following quoted list of 'Behavioural Symptoms' (Lusk and Waterman) it will be noticed that some of them will apply to children where deprivation (or privation) and emotional rejection was present over a long period — the sort of children introduced in chapter one — but where sexual abuse is not a factor. Some children showed 'acting out' behaviour:

- 'hostile — aggressive behaviour
  (although one small research project of six children, Shaw and Meier (1983) found their children to be **less** aggressive than normal)
- antisocial behaviour
- delinquency (with school-aged children)
- stealing
- tantrums
- substance abuse (including alcohol and drugs), with older children'

On the other hand some children, in the works studied by Lusk and Waterman, showed 'behaviours indicating withdrawal':

- withdrawal into fantasy
- staying inside and refusing to leave
- regressive behaviours (and return to thumb sucking, fear of the dark, a fear of strangers)

These authors also noted 'self-destructive' behaviours and 'self-hate' behaviour.

We can see how difficult it is to assess, only on the strength of these symptoms, whether or not a child has been (is being) sexually abused. Children can, however, be enabled to give other indicators, but this is not the place to enter into a full discussion concerning the assessment of sexual abuse.

People who are caring for children, especially where there is a known background of deprivation, rejection, cruelty, or behaviour problems, such as we have listed above, may expect to find more specifically indicative behaviour as was described in chapter one concerning Judy. Despite the fact that some children become sexually inhibited, wanting to hide their bodies and exhibiting shy sensitivity when some subjects come up in discussion, many children become sexualised, that is to say they show too great an interest in sexual matters, they often want to play games which involve imitations of adult sexual behaviour, as did Tony, Judy's brother:

> 'The whole thing made Mrs. Burrows "ill" and Mr. Burrows distracted. The family was being destroyed. Then there were the neighbours, and the neighbour's children. There was a terrible shindy the time nice Mrs. Harper found Tony lying on top of her six year old daughter and trying to put his "willie" up her.'

This **sexualised** behaviour is widely reported in the various studies made on children who have been sexually abused. Sometimes quite young children, months (or even a year or so) after being placed with foster parents, will come out with little descriptions of adult behaviour which no four or five year old would be expected to know about. This sort of talk is easily overlooked or dismissed especially as sometimes the child misinterprets some aspects of adult behaviour. In one case known to me the four-year-old girl spontaneously, when involved in play, told her foster mother how "daddy used to cry when Mummy sucked his willie". There had been various developmental and behavioural problems with this child, but each of those could be attributed also to poor nurture and emotional deprivation.

There is evidence, also, that as adolescents and adults, some sexually abused children may become 'promiscuous' or may experience sexual dysfunction (Brooks, 1982: Brunold, 1964; Jehu, 1988).

This book is called *If Only Someone Had Told Me,* and its main objectives are to tell caregivers, potential caregivers and others concerned with the care and training of children and young persons, about the background experiences their children are likely to have had, together with the effects these may have on the children, and to help people to relate in the most appropriate way to the children whatever disturbing behaviour, and disturbing stories they may come out with. For this reason we have given some straightforward descriptions, and used the expressions the children have used. People caring for these children must in the first place give the child the benefit of any doubt and **believe** (or accept) what the child is saying, and they should always be ready for new **revelations.** Indicators of previous sexual abuse, for example, may come out only after the child has become settled into the foster family — or even only after being adopted. This means that if they are people who feel they cannot 'cope' with this sort of thing, like the Burrows couldn't cope (Judy and Tony, chapter one) then they really should not become foster or adoptive parents — so now, if you are thinking about it, think some more because someone **has** told you!

Before closing this sub-section, here is a quote that will help us to bear in mind the different reactions, in broad terms, not as regards individual children, that sexual abuse may have on a child depending upon her developmental age. The quote is taken from a monograph by Mark Chesterman (1985):

> 'Therefore attention is drawn to the need to consider both incest types and developmental age in assessing the effects of incest. Goodwin and Owen (1982) were thus able to identify various problems that seemed related to age and developmental level. Up to 4 years the child may lose her toilet training, fear men, show disturbed sleep patterns and cling to the mother. In the range 4-6 years, it is usually a physical problem that brings the abuse out into the open — the child rarely makes a verbal complaint. During the latency age range phobias and physical complaints (particularly stomach pains) are common, as is a decline in school performance and general levels of interest. Adolescent victims may run away from home or become involved in other 'grand' gestures, for example, delinquency or attempted suicide. And victims who only tell when they are adults frequently manifest suicide or depressive gestures and experience problems in their relationship with others.'

Finally, most of these symptoms (eg. stomach pains) occur under so many different conditions that readers are asked never to jump to conclusions but to be watchful, thoughtful, and open with all child care workers. Remember, the damaging lumber in these cases (i.e. children with disturbed family backgrounds) is likely to include the most painful emotions concerning **betrayal** and the need for real affection, as well as something 'dirty', 'naughty' or 'terrifying'.

Tough luck!

In the following pages we shall look at certain childhood experiences which result from a blend of ignorance, carelessness, sickness and foolishness; together with the pressures resulting from poverty, the stress of modern western culture, economics, and controversial or even harsh **policies.** This conglomeration of factors, not all bearing down at once on particular families or individual children, accounts for a great deal of damaging lumber in the lives of children. Many children who finish up in long- term social care experience these pressures.

Just to give you an idea of what I am talking about — take 'ignorance and sickness'. I'm not sure whether either of these terms could fairly be applied to the case I am about to describe, but the reader will get the idea. I was involved with a thirteen- year-old boy whose mother had deserted the family and whose father had turned against the lad so that, as well as the actual loss of his mother and all the feelings (irrational feelings) of guilt he was carrying concerning her loss, he was also experiencing rejection by a father who told him that he was not macho enough.

Then, a few weeks after this miserable little thirteen-year-old came into care, his older sister whom he loved and clung to, but was well into alcohol dependency, was strangled — murdered. The boy's father visited him in a Children's Home and, not content with implying some responsibility for the girl's death, he entertained the child with lurid descriptions of what the girl had looked like when he'd seen her 'in the morgue'.

Perhaps the reader is able to imagine a little of the emotional pain carried by this boy. And just about the time all this was happening, members of parliament were pushing through a bill for making sure that parents and others would be able to exercise their 'rights' of **contact** (access) with the child. Having written that, I want to stress that I am one hundred per cent in favour of giving first priority to keeping families intact.

Nevertheless, we need a wisdom, a delicacy of approach, a **feeling,** understanding, approach to child care (and family care). We must not simply apply to every case whatever policy happens to be most fashionable, or economically advisable at the time ('controversial and even harsh policies'). I am reminded here of some words of Dr. Sula Woolff, Honorary Fellow in Psychiatry, University of Edinburgh (1987):

> 'While many parents with such personality features cope well, especially when supported by a warm and normally responsive marriage partner, some do not. Occasionally such parents lack all feeling for one of their children, or will see some special handicap or ill intent in a particular child, scapegoating and even persecuting this member of the family throughout his or her life.
>
> In my experience, when an injured or neglected child has such a parent, improvement is likely to be minimal. In my experience too schizoid/borderline personality traits are found in some parents who engage in very abnormal child care practices ------------ Prevention of separation in early life cannot be a global policy.'

Of course, many approaches should be available, including Family Therapy, but absolute rigidity of policy can also cause suffering and deprivation in children.

Children may suffer from the most subtle forms of damaging lumber, and very often the damage being done, or which has already been done to a child, is disguised to look like its very opposite and is presented to the courts, or to the media, as proof of affection and strong, protective bonding. Simon, aged fifteen now, is a child who is suffering in this way. His 'suffering' has gone on for years, and he has been gradually wedged into an emotional straitjacket. In some ways he reminds me of Morag (see Chapter One) who was obsessional about wanting everyone involved with her to be 'happy' all the time.

Simon has the same exaggerated need for absolute enduring peace between himself and everyone else in his life. But this can never be achieved and so he experiences enormous stress, especially as most of this energy is taken up with a sort of mental and verbal balancing trick in which he attempts, constantly, to mediate in all the clashes of personality and the demands of life. To make matters worse — much worse — his parents and many relatives and friends are definitely unstable. Worst of all is his mother who, as well as being agoraphobic and hypochondriacal has always been neurotically over-possessive with Simon.

This combination meant that Simon's development was peculiar, and painful, and frustrating. Most toys were seen as dangerous because of various 'things' which may emanate from them, either poisons from the paint or 'magnetism' of some kind. Simon was never allowed to play sporty games, nor was he allowed to 'play out' as the other children did in his street. Both parents constantly drilled into Simon, as he grew up, that he was fortunate to have such loving, kind, thoughtful parents.

At fourteen the child was a mess. Part of him rebelled; part of him continued to worship Mum and Dad — that is to say in a ritualistic way. Part of him hated Mum; part of him believed she had been his salvation and wanted almost to be part of her. At fifteen Simon hit his mother when she had almost driven him mad. He felt so terrible afterwards that he ran away from home. This sort of thing went on for months. Later, however, in the juvenile court, his parents were complimented on being 'model 'parents and, as the magistrate said, it was 'clear to everyone that Simon really loves his parents'.

Sometimes children are subtly controlled by 'double-bind' messages from their parents or other caregivers. I remember a thirteen-year old girl whose mother, separated from her husband, the girl's father, used to control her in this way. Doreen frequently truanted from school in spite of promises she made - to the teachers and the school welfare authorities. Doreen's whole life seemed to be full of contradictions — she was declared to be thoroughly **unreliable.**

The sort of thing that had been going on — for years — was typified in the double-bind message Doreen's mother gave her concerning school attendance. The mother herself had, three times, been hospitalized for attempted suicide. The message she gave to Doreen went like this:

> 'Doreen, you're a naughty girl — you're wicked — here's me in trouble with the school attendance (Officers) because you won't go to school. Get dressed and go, go on. Honestly, you'll kill me ----- you'll be the death of me yet ----- anyway what've I got to live for ----- you'll come home from school one of these days and find me lying on the floor — dead. Go on, off you go to school.'

This is a 'double-bind' message. It gives two separate messages. It says 'go to school because the law says so' and 'don't go to school, and if you do I'll kill myself'. The poor child is therefore in the wrong, and carrying blame, whatever course she takes.

People, foster-parents and others, who are asked to care for children who have experienced this form of lumber, this psychological possessiveness, have a difficult but very worthwhile task to perform. They **must** ask for the background history which is going to help them understand what has been happening to the child .They are likely to find themselves caring for a child with many obsessions, who fantasises, who has an ambivalent (loving-hating) attitude towards people, who carries many anxieties, and who feels full of guilt concerning parents or relatives who brought them up in this way. The guilt feelings will be telling the child 'you shouldn't be here, you **should** be with your mum and dad who've done so much for you.' Let me hasten to add that most people carry **some** of the characteristics listed above. It is a matter of **degree,** and the extent to which they cripple the child (or adult) or turn him into a very unhappy or violent or withdrawn person, which puts them into a different category.

Sometimes the **unwisdom** of weak, or rejecting, or overstressed parents subjects the child to additional psychological strain involving loneliness or feelings of failure to live up to the parents' image of what a **loveworthy** son or daughter should be. Some parents have a fixed idea of what they want their boy or girl to be like, or they have role models for boys and separate ones for girls so that a father may actually tell his little lad that he's 'useless' because he is no good at football. And if he turns out to be a boy with an artistic bent and a lot of sensitivity — who could even compose **poetry,** 'God forbid', then the child may feel that he is not only unloveworthy but odd — 'sissy'.

Some children need to grow up slowly, and in any case they may already be damaged to the extent that much of their play and social accomplishments fall behind their chronological age. Suffering already from **loss** or **rejection** or poor nurturing, the **stuck** child may need to play in a 'babyish' way, she may love to play with younger children and join in their games but will be told to 'act your age, will you'. The trouble is that her developmental age, at least in some aspects, may be well short of her chronological age.

Often children get **punished** in a way which serves to re-inforce feelings of rejection or, particulary with pre-school children, they suffer experiences which are terrifying. the child may be 'sent to bed' or sent to his room and left there, alone, cut off and apparently not wanted. Apart from encouraging feelings of rejection, or **confirming** that 'they hate me' this sending away (unless it is only for a few minutes, or one of the caregivers stays with the child) generates a deeper resentment and smouldering anger in some already damaged children. The reader will remember the child Vivien who was introduced in chapter one, and whose letter to her step-mother and dad included:

> 'I am runin away from here becors yous orl hate me. Anyhow I hat yous to and I am fed up with yous getting at me and me getting locked in me room -----'

With some quite young children the **punishment** includes fear as well as rejection. They may be locked in rooms, or even locked in dark cupboards, or actually tied to pieces of furniture.

Loss

Apart from the problem of space in a book of this sort we might quite easily have found reasons for a whole chapter on **loss.** As it is we shall have to limit our observations to this subsection and encourage our readers to follow up with further study.

By the term **loss** we are intending to understand the loss of another important person in the life of the child. But **loss** here is almost a generic term and is intended to include different sorts of loss, all involving the separation of the child from another person or persons where there has developed some degree of attachment and bonding.

This subject of **loss** must be seen as very important for those caring for children who have experienced deprivation and possibly subsequent forms of social care in Children's Centres (residential care) or foster homes. Our reason for emphasising the importance of **loss** in this respect is that the later caregivers (adopters, foster parents etc.) may be caring for children who have previously been wrongly treated concerning their experience of **loss** and the sequelae. So let us first see what we mean by loss within the context of our subject.

Bereavement would mean the loss of a person, and for a child to lose an attachment figure may be very traumatic, but children in long-term care are likely to have suffered other forms of loss. For example, the fact that the child is in care is likely to mean that she is physically separated from her parents even if they are both alive. The parents may have deserted, they may have 'put the child into care' **voluntarily** or, under more recent legislation, asked for the child to be 'accommodated', on account of some practical problem such as homelessness.

However, we can go a stage further with **loss.** Let us suppose that the child did experience actual bereavement in the case of one parent and loss by desertion in the case of the other parent. She goes to a Children's Centre to be temporarily cared for and assessed. In theory she is going to be there for three months, six at the most. But at **her** age (9? 11?) and with her 'problems' who wants to foster her? So she's still there eighteen months later. What she has done, however, is to form a relationship with a member of staff (with several members in fact) and attachment, along with a sense of security has developed. Not a very strong attachment but there all right.

Let's suppose the main failure in that particular centre was that nobody had the time to help the child to really **mourn** the loss of her parents. They did deal a bit with the death of her mother, but not enough. The father who had deserted was not thought of as a figure to be mourned, even though inwardly the child grieved about him.

This child at last goes into a foster home. She presents problems after a bit of a 'honeymoon' period. She also hints that she needs to talk about her losses. They amount to her mother, father, baby sister **and** two special members of staff at the centre. The practice of this particular foster family however, is to 'help her to **forget** those unhappy events'. After fifteen months the social services department is asked to move the child. Despite the problems experienced at the foster home this child may well have made a meaningful relationship with one or more members of the family — further **loss** experience!

A most salutary experience is to examine the placement history of a group of **in-care** older children; children up to the age of thirteen, but including children of eight or nine in the group. The number of moves, (of **placements**) some of the children have experienced is truly appalling in terms of child care and of **loss** experience. Don't forget that loss experience is only one effect of all these moves. There are also feelings of failure, feelings of rejection, anger feelings, and many others. But **loss** experience is likely to include, in the first place, the feelings and symptoms associated with **depression.**

Some children in public care are actually damaged by the sysem itself. The damaging lumber, apart from other things, may include as many as twenty moves in the life of a child not yet twelve years old. This is not an exaggeration, the author would be able to name two dozen children who have had over ten placements, some as many as twenty (at least one of twenty seven). Sometimes there are no interested or suitable natural parents in the case; sometimes **all** parents are treated as suitable and the child goes back and forth between 'home' and **various** placements, never being able to attach; never being able to cope with the multiplying experiences of **loss.** We would urge all prospective foster parents to give further thought to the help these children need, and to the nature of **loss,** including bereavement, and the way a child's personality may be affected by **loss.** Remember, that a child may come to you carrying unresolved, unexpressed feelings concerning **loss,** together with expectations, fears, anxieties (often proving fatally true) for the future. That is why we must be so sure of what we are taking on. That is why at least we must treat the whole matter of child caring as something almost sacred. Berridge and Cleaver (1987) discussing their findings concerning foster home breakdown emphasise the effects on the children, some of whom were 'highly distressed' and this was reflected in violent behaviour, delinquent acts, depression or deep withdrawal. As one youth explained when interviewed:

> 'I just went to pieces after I left the Gibsons. I really trusted that couple. The thing that hurt me most was that I thought it was going dead good and then they suddenly turned round and said they'd changed their minds and didn't want to foster. I really went mad when I got to Shorelands. I never realized I had a temper like that before it all came out, and I just wanted to destroy everything. My world had fell apart.'

To be fair, in my experience the moves do not usually come out of the blue in this way. Usually there are many complaints made, may be on both sides, and a lot of 'warnings' and promises of 'fresh starts', but it is also true that the same child with a **different couple** would have survived and changed.

So much more could go under the general headings of **tough luck** and **loss** — the sort of 'unfortunate' life experiences some kids have. Some are born into families in which the adults are constantly at loggerheads and use verbal and physical violence towards each other. Sometimes the boot is literally on the 'other' foot. Some children 'start life' with a bad birth experience which has an immediate adverse effect on them both as regards behaviour (eg. 'irritable' baby) and as regards feelings (stress and trauma) with spin-off onto the relationship between the child and parents. **Tough Luck** is usually a combination of factors, some of them inherent and others external to the child, and the way these factors interact.

The jigsaw puzzle

We have seen in Chapter One the kind of children we are concerned with. In Chapter Two we considered the missed-out experiences which are quite **precious,** in the best sense of that term — i.e. highly valuable. Precious, yet usually taken for granted by those of us who have them. In this chapter we have concentrated upon the sort of experiences our children should **not** have.

Of obvious interest to those of our readers caring for children who have had such unhappy starts to their lives as we have described, are the questions: Can we really act in such a way as to overcome the negative effects of these poor starts? Can we replace the missing life experiences? Can we counteract the effects of the many moves, the inconsistent care, the abuse and the ill-fortune? And if the short answer to these questions is 'yes', then how do we achieve these aims?

Because of its limited size, this small book cannot cover these questions, nor can it contain chapters on how those aims might be met — but we believe that the short answer to all the questions posed above is indeed 'yes'. Yes, we an counteract the ill-effects of their previous experiences, and yes — we can provide the missing experiences.

This is not to say that it will be easy to do these things. So many of these children are like 'broken' jigsaw puzzles. Not only is there a need for the separate pieces of the puzzle to come together, there is also the problem of pieces of the puzzle that are missing altogether, and there is the problem of sorting out the 'alien' pieces of the puzzle that don't belong at all!

Those who would parent these children back to **wholeness** will find that the jigsaw will not come together **only** with love, but nor will it truly come together without it. It will not come together without understanding, nor without patience, nor without disappointments and rejections. There is much to learn concerning the lost, exposed feelings generated in a child or young person who has previously learnt to defend his inner person by means of aggression and violence, but who has now reached a stage of being able to resist using violence.

Furthermore, those who would parent these children, and also those who really want to help them along the way and, maybe to see them back with their natural parents, will have so much to learn about their own feelings, their own prejudices, and their own fears. They will have so much to learn about their own weaknesses and strengths.

Where will people find the help they need in all this? One of the most fruitful sources of learning is to be found in the comparatively few 'tried and tested' 'good enough' foster parents, adopters of older children, or professional caregivers who can be recommended by the Social Services Departments or the Voluntary Societies. One can learn a lot by talking with them. There is also a growing number of professional child care social workers (residential and 'field') who are called upon by Training Officers in the child care agencies. These agencies must be urged to put on far more courses of training for caregivers.

Caregivers (foster parents, adopters, natural parents) will also need guidance and frequent consultations with specialist social workers, and sometimes child psychotherapists, paediatricians and others.

There is, however, an expanding range of specialist literature for those who wish to **understand** the problems and management of the disturbed child or young person. We have provided in our Further Reading section, a list of certain books and periodicals which could represent a start in earnest reading. The references we have made in the text (see Reference Section) will also guide the reader to a helpful source.

If the present small volume is read by prospective caregivers, our hope is that it will encourage and enlighten many, to the extent that children will benefit. But also, that those who might be helped to decide, rightly, against the role of caregivers to disturbed children will not need later on to say: *If only someone had told me!*

FURTHER READING

COMMENTS:

The books named and briefly described below have been found helpful to students, caregivers and various professionals. We have mostly kept away from advanced and complicated text books.

Most of the books were in print at the date of listing and should be obtainable from public libraries. Again, we have often given approximate prices which were applicable at the time of drawing up this list.

An excellent general guide to the literature is obtainable from the British Agencies for Adoption and Fostering. This guide is:-

'Family placement for children in care — a guide to the literature'
by Martin Shaw Price £9-95
Publisher: British Agencies for Adoption and Fostering, 1988
(address, end of section) ISBN 0-903534-74-6

Parenting

'A Good Enough Parent: A guide to bringing up your child'
by Bettleheim, B. Price £13-00 (hardback)
Publisher: Thames and Hudson, 1987 ISBN 0-500-01413-2

Bettleheim, the eminent child psychologist, who established and managed the famous Orthogenic School (for violent and highly disturbed adolescents) in Chicago wrote this book for parents, as a guide to child raising. Although his approach may still seem new and controversial to some, it is of proven value. A large book with 377 pages.

'Working With Children'

This book is described (below) under Personality Development, but many of the chapters outline attributes requisite for good-enough parenting.

'Adoption — The inside story,' Editor: Austin, J
Publisher: Barn Owl Books, 1985 ISBN 0-9509057-3-9

This interesting book is a collection of articles written by people who at the time were parenting children placed for adoption. As the blurb says, it reflects 'the problems, pains and pleasures which may face any adoptive family.

The problems may seem overwhelming at times, and the pain heartbreaking. But the pleasures can be tremendous.'

These accounts have come through the 'Parent to Parent Information on Adoption Services'.

'The Needs of Children' by Mia Kellmer Pringle
Publisher: Hutchinson, 2nd Edition 1980 (Paper)
ISBN 0-09-141331- 1

Although not specially about 'parenting' the various needs, as outlined here, lead to conclusions concerning parenting. A helpful, pragmatic, easy to understand book which, as well as spelling out emotional and attachment needs, contains chapters on, 'the parental and family role', 'consequences of failure to meeting children's needs' and 'children who are 'vulnerable' or 'at risk'.

'Living with a Hyperactive Child' by Wood, M.
Publisher: Souvenir Press (E & A) Ltd. 1984
ISBN (Paper) 0-285- 64987-6

As the title suggests, this book is about parenting **hyperactive** children. The author writes from personal experience with her hyperactive daughter, Tanya. A helpful, sympathetic yet practical book, written in biographical style. The author seems heavily committed to food allergy as a cause for hyperactivity, and therefore the following book is recommended as a balance.

'The Hyperactive Child — a parents guide'
described below under Personality Development.

'Mothering' by Schaffer, R. *Price £3.50*
Publisher: Fontana, 1977-85

This book describes for the lay reader aspects of child-parent interaction which in fact are very complex and could be studied at a highly technical level. It looks at the early, infantile, instinctive behaviour and at mothering as 'stimulation', concentrating also on the mother-child patterned interaction. Harder to understand than other books in this sub-section but **very** important.

'Long-Term Foster Care' by Rowe, J., et al

This book is described below under the sub-heading of Fostering, Fostering-Adoption Breakdown, Rehabilitation.

Fostering, Fostering-Adoption Breakdown, Rehabilitation

'The Child In Placement: Common Behavioural Problems'
by Fahlberg, V. Price £5.00
Publisher: BAAF (address, end of section)

'Helping Children When They Must Move'
by Fahlberg, V. Price £5.00

Publisher: BAAF, 1981 (address, end of section)
ISBN 0-903534-38x

This is a very practical guide for anyone involved in the care of children where **movement** from placement to placement is likely or has occurred. It contains training exercises.

'Adoption and Fostering — a practical guide'
by King, A.
Publisher: The Crowood Press, 1989 ISBN 1-85223-133-5

The author has written for 'prospective and existing' adoptive and foster parents. The book makes for easy reading and is well- informed. As the cover note states, the book deals with the emotional, financial, legal and 'practical' implications of caring for deprived children.

'Building New Families'
by Fitzgerald, J., et al. Price £7.00
Publisher: Basil Blackwell, Oxford, 1982
ISBN (paper) 0-631- 13193-0

The book describes work undertaken with children who at the time were 'in care'. It describes the way several children were helped to overcome the worst effects of emotional and social privation, and the planning and other techniques used when placing the children in new families.

'Good-Enough Parenting — A framework for assessment'
Edited by Adcock, M., and White, R. Price £6.00
Publisher: BAAF, 1985 (address, end of section)
ISBN 0-903534-57- 6

An excellent small book, although written, as the sub-title suggests, to help professional workers when assessing the child- rearing qualities of families, the book is an excellent guide for anyone wishing to learn about 'good-enough' parenting.

'Understanding Disruption'
by Fitzgerald, J. Price £3.25
Publisher: BAAF, 1983 (address, end of section)
ISBN 0-9035344-45- 2

This small book is both informative and practical (e.g. gives examples of techniques when working in fostering breakdown situation). It can be read with equal learning value by social workers and caregivers.

'Long-Term Foster Care'
by Rowe, J., Cain H., et al Price £10.00
Publisher: Batsford, 1984 ISBN (paper) 0-7134-5422-X

This book is intended more for the professional worker. It examines the placement experiences of 145 foster children. It looks at the families they were placed with and the factors causing breakdown. It contains some statistics.

Personality Development

'Child Development'
by Fahlberg, V. Price £5.50
Publisher: BAAF, 1982 (address, end of section)
ISBN 0-903534-40- 1

A compact, useful little book described as a 'workbook'. Fahlberg divides the book into six sections devoting the first to 'The First Year of Life, the fifth to 'Adolescence', and the sixth to 'special developmental issues'. Each of the first five sections looks at The Primary Task, Normal Development and Minimising the Trauma of Separation. The book contains exercises for discussion, etc.

'Working With Children'
Various contributors Price £6.00
Publisher: BAAF 1986 (address, end of section)

The book comprises a collection of papers which cover the developmental needs of children, and has sections on Attachment Theory, Intellectual Development, and Play. Developmental charts are included. A useful **introduction** to child development as an extra book.

Child Development — a first course'
by Sylva, K., and Lunt, J. Price £7.50
Publisher: Basil Blackwell, 1982-89 ISBN (paper) 86216-054-5

This useful introduction to the subject represents, as the title implies, a short course in its own right. It has a broad approach so that students are introduced to Piaget's work on the intellectual development, as well as to the attachment theory (a bit thin on this) and to Freudian ideas. It is a student's book rather than a popular reader.

'The Hyperactive Child — a parent's guide'
by Taylor , E. Price £4.00
Publisher: Martin Dunitz Ltd., 1985 ISBN 0-356-14492-5

This is one of the most helpful books ever written as a guide for parents, although most professional workers will also learn a lot from it. The writer is a medical specialist and is aware of the often 'conflicting and confusing' advice proffered on the subject. He gives a very balanced account of causes and treatment.

Sexual Abuse of Children

'Sexual Abuse of Young Children'
MacFarlane, K. et al. Price £16.00
Publisher: Holt, Rinhart & Winston, 1986 ISBN 0-03-910804-X

This book gives a broad introduction to the subject. It contains 15 chapters ranging from Chapter I, 'The Scope of the Problem' through to Chapter 4, 'Medical Evaluation' and on to Chapter 10 'Overview of Treatment Issues', and Chapter 11, 'Guidelines for Treating Young Children'.

This is a book for the ordinary intelligent reader whether employed professionally in children's work or otherwise involved in childcare, but it does go deeply into the subject.

Adoption and Fostering' Vol. 10., No. 3 (1986)
Published by (BAAF) (address, end of section)

A lot of space in this issue of the journal is devoted to child sexual abuse and there are special articles titled 'Child Sexual Abuse — The Power of Intrusion' and 'Telling Foster Parents about Sexual Abuse', but also there are useful articles on the prevention of foster home breakdown.

Child Sexual Abuse — Professional and Personal Perspectives'
by Peace, G., and McMaster, J. Price £7.75
Publisher: Boys' and Girls' Welfare Society, Schools Hill, Cheadle, Cheshire, U.K, 1989
ISBN 1-869801-06-7

This book forms part I of a three-part publication. Part I deals with aspects of investigation and is therefore good background reading for caregivers and other people likely to be involved with abused children. The book looks at the **administrative** problems of intervention as well as considering the degree of psychological damage associated with different forms of intervention. Difficult questions are posed, such as 'What effects might the medical examination have upon the child?'

'CHILD Sexual abuse — an interdisciplinary manual for diagnosis, case management and treatment'
by Faller, K.C. Price $10.00
Publisher: Macmillan, 1988 ISBN 0-333-49890-9

This is a rather more advanced book and is written with the professional worker in view. However, some specialist caregivers will find it very helpful. The book contains a chapter on 'Differential Diagnosis' which aims to classify types of sexual abuse (and abusers). There are chapters on 'Causes', 'The Assessment Process', 'Interviewing the Child', 'Interviewing the Perpetrator', 'Behavioural Characteristics and Physical Findings', etc.

The book has clear illustrations of the physical results of vaginal and anal penetrations.

The Senses — Sensory Healing

'Touching — the human significance of the skin' by Montagu, A.
Publisher; Harper & Row, 1971-78 ISBN 0-06-012979-4

Montagu impressively reminds readers about the importance of touch, perhaps indeed **awakening** some minds to the vital developmental aspect of touch and to the importance (as a tactile medium) of skin. An interesting work for anyone wishing to think deeper about child development and basic human needs.

'Windows to Our Children'
by Oaklander, V. Price $7.00
Publisher: Real People Press, 1978
(ISBN (paper) 0-911226-17-6

Although this book is written as a text book for people who are actually offering therapy to children it is extremely valuable as a means of learning about the importance of all the senses insofar as psychological development and mental health is concerned.

Child's Play': 'direct work' with the deprived child'
by Redgrave, K. Price £7.75
Publisher: Boys' & Girls' Welfare Society, Schools Hill, Cheadle, Cheshire. U(K. (1987) ISBN 1-869801-03-2

This book is concerned with therapy and counselling techniques which make use of 'third objects' (various materials, 'games' etc.) Chapter 4, however, concentrates on the need to enable some children to enjoy heightened 'sensory experiences' as one means of healing and obtaining psychosocial growth.

Attachment Theory

'Attachment and Separation'
by Fahlberg, V. Price £3.50
Publisher: BAAF, 1981 (address, end of section)
ISBN 0-903534-37- 1

This is a well recommended, small compact book which gives the basic theory as well as providing case examples in brief, exercises, and sections on 'separation', and 'Assessing Attachment'. The book expounds on the Arousal-Relaxation cycles.

'Child Development'
by Fahlberg, V.

Reviewed in sub-section (above) titled Personality Development, but recommended reading for attachment theory as well.

Chapter:
'The Making and Breaking of Affectional Bonds'
This chapter by Bowlby, J., appears in the book 'Working With Children' (reviewed above, in sub-section titled Personality Development).

Note: The following three-volume set of books represent more advanced reading:

'Attachment and Loss, Vol. 1. Attachment' price £8.00 each
'Attachment and Loss, Vol. 2. Separation'
'Attachment and Loss, Vol. 3. Loss'
All by Bowlby, J.
Publisher: Penguin 1971-89

Address of BAAF:
British Agencies for Adoption and Fostering
11 Southwark Street
London, SE1 1RQ

REFERENCES

Adams, C., & Fay, J., 1981 *'No more secrets: protecting your child from sexual assault'* Impact Publishers.

Ainswoth, M.D. & Boston, M. 1952, 'Psychodiagnostic Assessements of a Child after Prolonged Separation in Early Childhood' in *The British Journal of Medical Psychology.*, 25:169-201

Allen, A., and Morton, A., 1963 'This Is Your Child' Routledge & Kegan Paul London.

Aldgate, J. et al., 1988 'Direct Work with Children. A Guide for Social Work Practitioners' Batsford, London.

Bander, K.W. Fein, E., & Bishop, G., 1982 'Child Sex Abuse Treatment: Some Barriers to Program operation' *in Child Abuse and Neglect,* No. 6.

Berridge, D. and Cleaver, H., 1987 'Foster Home Breakdown' Basil Blackwell, Oxford and USA.

Bettelheim, B., 1987 'A Good Enough Parent' Thames and Hudson, London, UK.

Bowlby, J. 1986 'The Making and Breaking of Affectional Bonds' in *Working With Children.* British Agencies For Adoption and Fostering.

Brooks, B. 1982 'Familial Influence on Father-Daughter Incest' in Journal of Psychiatric Treatment and Education, 4, 117-124

Brunold, H. 1964 'Observations after Sexual Traumata suffered in Childhood' in *Excerpta Criminologica* (January-February) pp. 60-66

Buda, F.B. et al, 1972 'Hypotonia and the Maternal-Child Relationship' in *American Journal of Diseases of Childhood* 124, 906-907

Chesterman, M. 1985 'Child Sexual Abuse and Social Work' Social Work Monograph No. 33, University of East Anglia, Norwich, U.K.

Colwell, Maria. 1974 'The Report of the Committee of Inquiry into the Care and Supervision Provided in Relation to Maria Colwell' DHSS, London.

Community Care, 1988 Special Inset, 'Inside: working with Child Abusers' in Journal, *Community Care* 29th Sep. 1988.

Cooper, C., 1986 'The Growing Child' in *Working With Children*, Practise Series 13 (British Agencies For Adoption and Fostering)

Dunn, J., 1984 'Sisters and Brothers' Fontana, London.

Erikson, E.H. 1965 'Childhood and Society' Penguin Books Ltd.

Fahlberg, V. 1981 'Attachment and Separation' British Agencies for Adoption and Fostering.

Fahlberg, V. 1984 Training Pack 'In Touch With Parents' British Agencies for Adoption and Fostering.

Gates, Lucie. 1982 'Report of the Panel of Inquiry Appointed by the London Borough of Bexley, and Greenwich and Bexley Area Health Authority with Reference to Linda Gates and her family.'

Gaussen, T., 1984 'Developmental Milestones or Conceptual Millstones? Some Practical and Theoretical limitations in Infant Assessment Procedures' in Child Care, Health and Development, Vol. 10, No. 2., 1984 (Blackwell Scientific Publications)

Gibson, M.T. 1966 'What Is Your Favourite Thing to Hear?' Grosset and Dunlop U.S.A.

Glueck, S. and E., 1952 'Delinquents In The Making' Harper and Row, U.K.

Goodwin, J. and Owen, J. 1982 'Incest from Infancy to Adulthood' in *Sexual Abuse: Incest Victims and their Families*, Goodwin, J. (ed.) John Wright, Bristol, U.K.

Haste, H., and Bruner, J. S. 1987 'Making Sense', Methuen

Holmes, S.J. and Robins, L.N., 1987 'The Influence of Childhood Disciplinary Experience on the Development of Alcoholism and Depression', in *Journal of Child Psychology & Psychiatry* Vol. 12 No. 3

Hurlock, E.B. 1964 'Child Development' (4th Edit.) McGraw-Hill, Inc.

Jehu, D. 1988 'Beyond Sexual Abuse — Therapy with women who were childhood victims' John Wiley & Co.

Kempe, R.S., and C.H., 1978. 'Child Abuse' Fantana/Open Books, U.K.

Kennell, J. et al., 1976 'Parent-Infant Bonding' in *Child Abuse and Neglect*, Helfer R., and Kempe, C.H. (Eds) Cambridge, Mass: Ballinger Pub. Co.

La Fontaine, J. 1989 'Child Sexual Abuse: an ESRC Research Briefing' in *After Abuse*, British Agencies for Adoptions & Fostering.

Lowenfeld, M. 1964 'The Study of Preverbal Thinking and its Relation to Psychotherapy' Paper delivered to the Sixth International Congress of Psychotherapy. (Quoted by Margarital Wood in 'Art as Therapy' Dalley, T. Ed., 1984)

Lusk, R., Waterman, J. 1986 'Effects of Sexual Abuse on Children' in *Sexual Abuse of Young Children* MacFarlane, K., Waterman J. et al. Holt, Rinehart and Winston, London & Sydney.

Meadows, S. 1986 'Understanding Child Development' Hutchinson, U.K.

Montague, A., 1971 'Touching: The Human Significance of the Skin' Columbia Univ. Press.

Oaklander, V., 1978. 'Windows To Our Children' Real People Press, Moab, Utah, USA.

Pfeffer, C., Newcorn, J., et al. 1989. 'Subtypes of Suicidal and Assaultive Behaviors In Adolescent Psychiatric Inpatients — A Research Note' in *Journal of Child Psychology and Psychiatry* Vol. 30, No 1.

Redgrave, K. 1987 'Child's Play — Direct Work with the Deprived Child' Boys and Girls Welfare Society, Cheadle, Cheshire, U.K.

Richards, M.P.M. 1974. 'First Steps In Becoming Social' in *The Integration of the Child into a Social World*, Ed. M.P.M. Richards, Cambridge University Press, London, UK.

Rutter, M., 1975 'Helping Troubled Children' Penguin Books.

Scarpitti, F.R. et al., 1960 'The 'good' boy in a high delinquency area; four years later' in *American Sociological Review* 1960, 25, 555-558

Schaffer, H.R., 1985 'Making Decisions About Children' in Adoption and Fostering Vol. 9, No. 1, 1985 (British Agencies for Adoption and Fostering)

Schaffer, H.R., 1977 'Studies in Mother-Infant Integration' Academic press, London U.K.

Shaw, V.L. & Meier, J.H. 1983 'The Effect of Type of Abuse and Neglect on Children's Psychosocial Development' Unpublished manuscript, Children's Village, U.S.A.

Shirley, H.F. 1963 'Pediatric Psychiatry', Harvard Univ. Press Cambridge, Mass.

Smith, G. 1989 'Child Sexual Abuse: the Power of Intrusion' in *After Abuse*, British Agencies for Adoption and Fostering.

Storr, A. 1985 Bulletin No. 16. British Association of Psychotherapists.

Symonds, N. 1987 'The Secret Rose' Marshall Pickering, U.K.

Thom, M. 1984 'Working With Children: the Violet Oaklander approach' in *Adoption and Fostering,* No. 3. (British Agencies for Adoption & Fostering).

Triseliotis, John, 1983 'Identity and Security' in *Adoption and Fostering* Vol. 7, No. 1, 1983 (British Agencies for Adoption and Fostering)

Vale Allen, C. 1983 'Daddy's Girl' British Library (NEL Paperback) C.I.P

Waterman, J & Lusk, R. 1986 'Scope of the Problem' in Sexual *Abuse of Young Children* (as above, Lusk and Waterman)

Winnicott, D.W. 1968 'The Family and Individual Development' Social Science Paperbacks. Tavistock Publications, London U.K.

Winnicott, D.W. 1985 'Playing and Reality' Pelican Books (re- issue)

Woolff, S. 1987 'Predication in Child Care' in *Adoption and Fostering,* Vol. 11, No. 1 British Agencies for Adoption & Fostering.

FURTHER PUBLICATIONS FROM THE BOYS' AND GIRLS' WELFARE SOCIETY

GLUE SNIFFING AND SOLVENT ABUSE

by D J O'Connor

This informative and realistic book offers guidance and information in a practical style to all concerned with solvent abuse. Denis O'Conner, arguably the leading UK authority on glue sniffing and solvent abuse, established a clinic in 1978 and has treated thousands of young people since that time.

CHILD'S PLAY:
'Direct Work' with the Deprived Child

by Ken Redgrave

This illustrated, practical guide is helpful to all working with disturbed children, and describes various techniques and 'games' which act as indicators of a child's history and nuturing needs. Ken Redgrave has been working with children for over 35 years and possibly has a wider experience of child care work than most other social workers employed today.

FAMILY WORK IN RESIDENTIAL CHILD CARE:
Partnership in Practice

by John Kelsall and Billy McCullough

This book highlights an innovative and exciting approach to working with children in care, and provides agencies with practical ideas for sharing responsibility with families and developing more effective practice. John Kelsall and Billy McCullough are lecturers in Social Work with vast experience of working with families in a variety of residential settings.

TRUANCY AND SOCIAL WELFARE:
Bells Ringing in the Distance

by Godfrey Holmes

This book discusses truancy in a social work as well as educational context and gives an invaluable insight into the problems of and reasons for non-school attendance. Techniques and approaches to truancy are outlined providing the reader with increased skills, knowledge and awareness to tackle the problem effectively. Godfrey Holmes has been both a teacher and a social worker and is a regular contributor to a number of professional journals in social work and education.

CHILD SEXUAL ABUSE:
Professional and Personal Perspectives
Part 1: Aspects of Investigation

by Gillian Peace and John McMaster

The problems faced daily by professional agencies who are coping with children and families involved in suspected and proven sexual abuse in this text. The opinions, attitudes and ideas of managers through to front-line practitioners will be of keen interest to all those working in the field and will further the understanding of everyone concerned with this complex and disturbing problem. Gillian Peace has researched for many years in the social and medical field and John McMaster, Chief Executive of the Boys' and Girls' Welfare Society, is author and contributor to many texts on aspects of social and educational care.

CHILD SEXUAL ABUSE:
Professional and Personal Perspectives
Part 2: Interprofessional Collaboration

by Gillian Peace

'The key issues of child sexual abuse are clouded by strong feelings which lead to poor communication with agencies, professionals and clients. We need above all better communication to get the best care and help for children and families'.

This book examines why professionals have difficulty working together and why it is vital to overcome these difficulties when working in this field. It examines attitudes and opinions of managers through to front-line practitioners concerning the formal forum of the Area Child Protection Committee and the Case Conference, and collaboration between individual professionals with a focus on partnership initiatives. Suggestions for improving relationships are also explored.

The book will be of keen interest to all those working in the field and will further the understanding of everyone concerned with this complex and disturbing problem.

ALCOHOL AMONG YOUNG PEOPLE:
Obtaining the Full Measure

by Godfrey Holmes

This text confronts the issues of young people and drink within six main sections. It examines research findings, discusses the effects of alcohol on physical and mental health, explores young people's motives for drinking alcohol and suggests alternatives. The text gives an invaluable insight into the effects of extensive media promotion of alcohol and the difficulties in identifying solutions to the problem in the light of the general social acceptance of alcohol as a desirable substance. Godfrey Holmes has been both a teacher and a social worker and is a regular contributor to a number of professional journals in social work and education.

ORDER FORM

I would like to order the following texts:

		No. of copies
Glue Sniffing & Solvent Abuse	**£6.75**	☐
Child's Play	**£7.75**	☐
Family Work in Residential Child Care	**£7.75**	☐
Truancy and Social Welfare	**£7.75**	☐
Child Sexual Abuse: Part 1 Professional and Personal Perspectives	**£7.75**	☐
Child Sexual Abuse: Part 2 Interprofessional Collaboration	**£7.75**	☐
Alcohol Among Young People	**£7.75**	☐

The total cost of my order is .... and I enclose a cheque made payable to **Boys' and Girls' Welfare Society** for this amount.

Name ....

Address ....

Please send your order to Pauline Bruchez, Boys' and Girls' Welfare Society, Central Offices, Schools Hill, Cheadle, Cheshire SK8 1JE. Tel. 061-428 5256.